Looking Through the Prism

Navigating Life with a Visual Disability

THOMAS DANA

Looking Through the Prism
Navigating Life with a Visual Disability

Copyright © 2022 by Thomas Dana

All rights reserved. No part of this publication may be reproduced or transmitted in any form or by any means, electronic or mechanical, including photocopy, recording or information storage and retrieval methods now known or to be invented, without the written permission of the publisher, except by a reviewer who may quote brief passages in a review.

ISBN: 9798366683753

Book and cover design by Deanna Washington
Interior photos: All photos copyright Thomas Dana

Printed in the United States of America

To my immediate and extended family.

*To Jay Henderick, Larry Holsen,
and John Crane,
for friendship beyond expectations.*

CONTENTS

Foreword 7

Chapter 1. The Formative Years 11

Chapter 2. Oakland Tech 21

Chapter 3. College of San Mateo: Challenges, Disappointments, and Successes 30

Chapter 4. Santa Clara University and the Bronco Mascot Spirit . . . 35

Chapter 5. Struggle and Success: Earning My Teaching Credential 43

Chapter 6. Entering the World of Work: Finding the Right First Job 52

Chapter 7. Married Life and a Family 63

Chapter 8. Sacramento: The Rollercoaster Years 70

Chapter 9. A New Career Direction 75

Chapter 10. Transition: In the Desert 84

Chapter 11. My Life Enriched with Private Sector Employment . . . 90

Chapter 12. Another Transition 106

Chapter 13. Days of Wine and Roses in Napa. 113

Chapter 14. Retirement: The Golden Years 127

Chapter 15. A Coveted Job and the Opportunity of a Lifetime 136

Chapter 16. My Family: A Tribute 146

Chapter 17. The Psychology of Disability 160

Chapter 18. Coming Full Circle 172

Appendix: Agency Resources 180

Acknowledgments 182

About the Author 187

Foreword

People with sensory, physical, and mental disabilities live within what I call the "prism of disability." We face challenges due to our disability, and challenges of our own making, as well as misconceptions, bias, and overprotectiveness from others. Even in today's world, bigotry and fear of people who are different from us still create social divisiveness. It is imperative to counteract these challenges, and hearing the life stories of successful disabled people can help the nondisabled become aware of what is possible and reveal ways in which the disabled and the abled are alike.

At the age of seventy-six, and having been retired for ten years, I want to share my story, because time is of the essence. I hope this story will enhance awareness for those who live with a disability (or disabilities), and for people who struggle with, or have no understanding of how to live side by side with, people with physical or mental impairments.

In 1944, I was born two months premature and weighed only three pounds. I was put in an incubator to receive the oxygen necessary to keep me alive. This preventive procedure caused blindness or severe vision loss in approximately ten thousand babies born between the early 1940s and mid-1950s. The medical term for this condition is Rentro-lento-fibroplasia (RLF) or Retinopathy of Prematurity (ROP).

Most people assume a blind person has no vision at all. But there are degrees of blindness. In my case, I am legally blind, and though I have some vision, I cannot see what a normal sighted person sees. My vision is minimal at or below 20/400, the cutoff point for being legally blind.

I have no depth perception. I can see people when they are in range of my minimal vision. But without depth perception, I can trip over objects that a sighted person would easily see. At times I have been walking down a street, gearing up to say hello to an oncoming pedestrian, only to be shocked to encounter a light pole that has not been moving even an inch.

When I am talking with you, I can see the form of your body but not the color of your eyes or the expression on your face. If your voice sounds harsh, but you wear a smile, I would not see it. I can see colors when I am close to an object. I cannot see the object as clearly as a sighted person, but I can distinguish one color from another.

Someone who is totally blind has no vision at all. Over time, based on conversations with other people, a blind person comes to associate the names of colors with certain objects. For example, yellow sun; red fire engine; blue sky or lake; green Christmas tree; red, white, and blue flags; and so forth. The blind person's imagination compensates for their lack of visual cues.

Without depth perception, cars of the same shape or color look alike. Many times, I have assumed I had a clear path to a vehicle that had brought me to my destination and was waiting to pick me up. To my surprise, I found myself trying to enter the wrong car, to the sometimes unkind protests of the driver.

Once, when I was exploring the grounds of a school I had attended many decades earlier, I reached down to pet what I thought was a small, friendly dog. It was a skunk. On the bus and streetcar rides home, I listened as people wondered about the skunk smell, assuming it came from outside the bus or streetcar.

My other senses are highly attuned to my environment, and I try to compensate for the lack of sight as best I can. I read Braille, but I cannot read a printed page from a book or newspaper. I cannot tell you how many times I have been in a restaurant and asked the server to read portions of the menu to me, only to experience profound surprise when the bill arrived, because I had forgotten to ask about prices.

On a humorous note, a number of years ago I was riding a Greyhound bus from Santa Cruz to San Jose, California. Greyhound drivers were on strike at the time and some of the backup drivers seemed not to have received appropriate training. On the road to San Jose, the driver asked if someone could direct him to the San Jose bus station. When I volunteered, people saw my white cane as I walked to the front of the bus, and I'm certain they wondered how I could safely direct the driver. But I had traveled from Santa Cruz to San Jose surely over a hundred times, so I knew which turnoff and roads to take. As we traveled down Highway 17, I barked out directions to the driver, repeating them frequently. When we arrived at the station, I received many words of thanks and appreciation for my efforts.

At a certain point in my career, I knew in my heart that my life's work was to promote and support academic and job accessibility for students with disabilities. My story focuses on that journey, and its trials and triumphs. Although my successes and failures were impacted by my lack of visual acuity, these challenges empowered me to find solutions and spur of the moment strategies to achieve my goals, in spite of circumstances.

I tell my life story in this book not because what I accomplished was anything special, but rather to support the uniqueness of people with disabilities, celebrate our accomplishments and victories, and lay foundations of awareness and hope for those in the next generation and beyond.

I will be happy if you take from this book just one idea or story that influences you to act or react differently or that challenges you in some way in your relationship with your disability or in your interaction with a disabled person.

Throughout this book, I have used fictional names of students and often of other people.

In the Appendix is a list of agencies and programs that serve people with disabilities locally and nationally.

Chapter 1

The Formative Years

My entire life has taken place in a period during which the world has been in a state of flux. In 1944, my birth year, the Atomic Age was on the verge of setting a new agenda for the world. Even though the extended family was still intact, the transition into the nuclear world after World War II had a profound effect upon the family structure in our society.

When I was growing up, our whole family—aunts, uncles, and cousins—went to Grandma Dana's house for birthday celebrations and special dinners. This gave us all an opportunity to reinforce our relationships with all the members of our family. As the years passed, however, as the nuclear age advanced and society adapted to new challenges ranging from diversity issues to an expanding global economy, we lost the family and social foundation that had enhanced people's lives from cradle to grave.

Growing up in this changing environment, I thought I was having a normal childhood. My parents and siblings loved me, I played outdoors with friends, and I never felt different from others. However, this changed when my parents enrolled me in first grade at the Sunnybrae School in San Mateo, California, in the fall of 1950.

I knew before I went to school that something was wrong with my vision, because we had regularly visited the ophthalmologist's office in San Francisco. In first grade, it became apparent from the start that I would experience problems in and outside the classroom. The teacher routinely asked us to look up and read what was on the blackboard. I could see the board was a beautiful shade of green, but I could not see the letters and words printed on the board.

I was ridiculed and called "cross-eyed" by kids who did not understand why one of my eyes was smaller than the other and had a white cataract. Some children would hit or shove me. Except for my eye, I was a normal looking kid, with dark brown wavy hair, brown eyes, and a slightly tan complexion from my father's Italian heritage. Later in life I would understand that many children have difficulties being accepted into a social group of their peers. However, at six years old, I knew only that others perceived me as different because of my vision loss.

As I moved through the stages of my life, a sense of inadequacy and not being good enough at whatever I tried to do would hang over me like a wet blanket. The process of building self-esteem and confidence took years. When I began to think of myself as a person first, regardless of my disability, I realized that having a disability was not the primary factor preventing me from moving forward.

As the new decade of the 1950s materialized, parents of children with disabilities faced many unpleasant realities when it came to securing an education for those children. There were residential schools and institutions for the blind, deaf, and developmentally disabled, but there were no classes within the public school system for students with special needs. It would be another quarter century before Federal legislation would guarantee certain educational rights to these children. In 1975, the Individuals with Disabilities Education Act (DEA) provided that framework in the form of individualized education plans (IEPs), which designated support services and other assistance to students in the K through 12 system.

My parents did not want to send me to a boarding school at such a young age. So, they and other parents who faced the same dilemma petitioned local county education departments to establish special resource classes. In the fall of 1951, the county set up two special resource classes for partially sighted and severely blind students and hired special education teachers at the Lawrence School, a public school in San Mateo. By 1955, resource classes for children with special needs were established at two other schools in San Mateo County (McKinley Grammar and Fair Oaks Grammar schools). I attended all three schools in my first few years of education.

Initially, my parents hoped I could attend a public school if I was taught Braille and learned how to use a print typewriter, a now antiquated version of a Braille typewriter (called the Perkins Brailler). The device had six keys, a line spacer, a back spacer, and a paper roll, just like an old manual typewriter. Today, the visually impaired use a regular computer keyboard equipped with Braille keys, or screen-reader listening software, to access the printed word. In the 1950s, we grew up using the print typewriter as our primary way to communicate with the sighted world.

The idea of teaching disabled children in a segregated classroom with a special research teacher became a primary foundation of learning in the public schools. In an integrated classroom, instructors would not have time to provide the one-on-one attention needed by students with physical and sensory disabilities. In these segregated classrooms, we learned spelling, math, and reading, as well as practical skills such as raising rabbits and canaries.

However, this protective environment did not provide the diversity of direct interaction with non-disabled students. The only time we were invited to sit in on a regular class was when the teacher offered a reading session or we could take a spelling quiz using a Perkins Brailler. For me, these visits to a regular classroom were forays into a world of mystery and insecurity, and I and other blind students experienced many learning challenges. In fifth grade, for example, I would draw with crayons while others were reading silently or working on other projects. The only time I felt part of the integrated classroom was when I took spelling tests along with the other students by writing my answers with a Braille device. I then took the finished test back to the resource instructor for review and a grade. When my grades indicated minimal progress, my parents reluctantly decided to enroll me in a special school, where I would spend the next seven and a half years.

It was a cold windy day in January of 1957 when my mother drove me to the California State School for the Blind in Berkeley, California. The school was home to about 160 students, girls and boys, in grades one through nine. There were two dormitories, a two-story building that housed administrative offices and classrooms, a gymnasium, an infirmary staffed by round-the-clock nurses, and two houses occupied variously by the school superintendent, an employee, or faculty. The boys' dorm, Wilkinson's Lodge, or WL as we called it, sat on a hill overlooking the Bay and the campus in the beautiful Berkeley Hills, just south of the University of California. The school grounds featured green fields, trees, a baseball field, and a playground with swings and slides. Our school was next to a school for the deaf, which had a campus twice as large.

My room, on the second floor of the dorm, was sunny, with individual lockers and a place to hang clothes and store personal items. I met my roommate and dorm counselor on the day I arrived. As my mother helped me unpack and oriented me to my surroundings, I felt excited to begin this new phase of my life. As my mother said goodbye, however, both of us grew tearful, knowing that a major change had just occurred in our lives.

I soon realized I had much in common with my peers. All of us had visual impairments, we missed our families, and we wanted to do as well as we could at learning, so we could someday return home to be with our family and friends.

But there were also non-similarities. All of us had different family upbringings, and a number of students had behavioral problems. The dormitory environment was at times challenging and difficult, and the dorm staff could not be everywhere at once. I was physically tormented and beaten up for no reason by stronger and heavier students. At age twelve-and-a-half, I was of normal build—neither skinny nor overweight—and about 130 pounds. You had to take the slaps and the punches, because if you did not, there would be repercussions.

As I grew stronger through the excellent physical education program coordinated by Dr. Charles Buell, who was himself partially sighted, I could eventually hold my own against subsequent threats. I am eternally grateful to Dr. Buell for teaching us young and adolescent boys to become skilled in wrestling, swimming, and track and field. We even wrestled local high school teams and won many victories. Not to sound too modest—I won two-thirds of my matches, with a record of 42 victories and 21 losses.

Life in the dormitory had its ups and downs. The building was old (built in the early twentieth century) and reeked of odors related to dirty bathrooms and cleaning fluids. The steam heaters hissed and clanged. Janitors waxed the hallways and our bedroom floors with a noisy machine at least twice a week. The smell of wax was ever present. On the lower floor, next to the laundry room, the dorm counselor washed clothes and sheets, and repaired ripped or torn clothing.

When I first arrived, meals were served in the dormitories. A year later, a cafeteria building was constructed that accommodated 155 students and 30 staff. No matter where the meals were served, we students abhorred the institutional food, except for the ice cold milk from the milk machine. To be fair, the food improved at the annual

Christmas dinner just before we left for the holidays, and we were thrilled to be served a traditional turkey with all the trimmings. We were fond, too, of the hot buttered toast for breakfast, served in stacks of about ten. Whoever got the top two slices from the stack had the superb advantage of biting into a fresh piece of toast that was not soggy or burned.

It bothered me that I would see my family and neighborhood friends only on weekends or holidays. I longed for a normal life like other kids.

There were also unthinkable incidents that to this day are likely still talked about by those who experienced them. Some dorm counselors were impatient and yelled at the kids. One counselor went into the dorm rooms at night and sexually abused older students. This happened to me several times when lights were out in the quiet of the evening. Had I not had a roommate, I would have experienced even more despair. I knew my roommate was not asleep and I also knew he was too scared to fight off a 200-pound man. We agreed not to report the incidents because we feared the perpetrator's behavior would get worse instead of better. It went on for a few months. My roommate told me afterward how horrible he had felt at the time and wished there was something he could do.

I fought off these unwelcome gestures as best I could, but psychological damage was done. In the late 1950s and early 1960s, such abnormal behaviors were not openly discussed. You rarely heard about homosexuality or child abuse, or even about social discrimination unless it referred to Black people. If I had complained to the school superintendent, would he have believed me? Or would the abuse have increased? Instead, I repressed the events as best I could.

Many years later, I told my mother, who of course was shocked. I bring it up here only to document that life at the school posed challenges other than disability issues, and I believe these experiences delayed my personal and social development. Only when I was much older did I deal with these issues in therapy and by talking with close friends.

Things at the school did not always go so well in the classroom, either. Many instructors had good intentions and did their best to teach the elementary and middle school curriculums. Training in the use of Braille and typing proved excellent preparation for future academic endeavors. I am still a Braille user, and if I had never learned to use a print typewriter, I would have a hell of a time using a computer today.

However, when it came to English, math, and foreign languages, certain teachers had no business instructing special needs students, and I believe it's fair to say that their attitudes negatively impacted an entire generation of students. These teachers played favorites and assisted only students who were gifted or could catch on quickly. Many students, myself included, were rarely called on in a math or language classroom because we were slow learners or not the teacher's pet. It's possible the school principal and superintendent had no idea what was going on.

It was only a number of years after I graduated that I discussed these issues with other students and with some faculty who had witnessed this unprofessionalism. As for myself, I had great difficulty with math courses in high school and college, because I had not received the necessary concepts and foundations to be successful in advanced math classes.

In a sense, when you attend a boarding school, you grow up more quickly because you do not have parents and siblings to fall back on for support. Even though I experienced problems in school and beyond, the adversity I experienced at the School for the Blind challenged me to work harder and not feel sorry for myself. There were several teachers I grew to respect and love for their dedication to our education, and more importantly, for their emphasis on teaching us about habits, values, and attitudes we would need as adults. For example, math problems could teach us how to use a budget to pay bills; history lessons could discuss what it takes to be an effective leader or public servant.

Among the teachers who had tremendous impact on my life and who deserve high praise for their efforts to support students in educational and life challenges was Mrs. Nunes, my sixth grade teacher. Compassionate, objective, and wise, she challenged us to learn and to develop as young people.

Mrs. Wright-Groelle was the school librarian. Liz, as I now call her, was always available to listen and offer advice on how to resolve personal problems constructively. At the end of each spring semester, she offered us part-time jobs to help her reorganize the school library before summer vacation. Not only did we have fun completing the tasks, but she took us to lunch or dinner afterward at a restaurant we liked. She didn't tolerate my complaints about how tough life was, how I had trouble retaining information, or how inadequate I felt socially.

At first, I perceived her as picking on me. But in reality she was trying to get me to think more objectively and not be so hard on myself. Now we are close friends and often attend symphonies together and share meals in excellent restaurants. Liz recently turned ninety-one and is still active in her church and professional organizations. She was a strong force in my life who not only challenged me but was always there for me during illness and at the high points of my education, such as attending my graduations from high school and college.

I doubt I would have any interest in history had it not been for Mr. English, my junior high history and English instructor. Mr. English constantly challenged us to remember important historical dates. He read us engaging stories about memorable events such as the conspiracy to assassinate Abraham Lincoln and the life of King Henry the Eighth, who successfully opposed the Pope over a divorce issue and became head of the new Church of England. Mr. English, as well as Mr. Salzberry, our typing instructor, were favorites among all the students.

Finally, Mr. George Foggerty was a jolly fellow full of humor who taught economics and business. During eighth grade, his Business Practices class gave us opportunity to learn how to operate a candy stand that was open on weekday afternoons at the school. We learned to obtain supplies, count money and make change, and explain the available inventory to prospective customers. At the end of each week we would prepare a profit report in Braille, then go to the school business manager and dictate this report to him. At the end of the year, profits from candy sales were divided among the students in the program. I was thrilled to receive a check for almost twenty-five dollars before I left for summer vacation. At that time, twenty-five dollars could buy a good hamburger and plenty of long-playing records.

The complex at 3001 Derby Street was our temporary home, and as I have shared, tremendously impacted our lives as young students tackling issues that would lead to our successes and failures as adults. What stands out for me about life at the School for the Blind is how challenging it was to live in a dormitory with students whose origins were different from my own. They came from Los Angeles and San Diego and all over California.

One of my best friends was from Mexico. He had suffered an eye injury and his mother moved to California with two small boys for his eye surgery. However, he remained almost totally blind. Another friend was from San Francisco; he could play the piano and was popular and talented and succeeded at everything he tried. Then there was a Hispanic student from southern California, who was mean and finally expelled for badly beating up an always friendly and gifted classmate who could play the piano after just hearing the music from a record or another pianist.

Most of us were lucky enough to have supportive parents or an extended family who accepted our differences without question or negativity. Two or three times I took a roommate home to visit my family on the weekend. My parents and my siblings, Paul and Marianne, extended a warm hospitality, and my friends enjoyed my mother's cooking. Once, my father invited a friend and me to help him plant an apple tree in the back yard.

Chapter 2

Oakland Tech

After completing ninth grade at the School for the Blind, most of us continued to live at the school and attended nearby Oakland Tech high school. Others attended the local Berkeley High School or returned to their home communities to complete high school there. Those who attended their hometown schools would be assisted by resource teachers who provided Braille and large-print course materials, as well as community volunteers (called "readers") who read course materials aloud to blind students.

One benefit of remaining at the School for the Blind was its special reader support program in the evenings. This program was administered by Robert Campbell, who was blind and had built his own home in the Berkeley hills. The sighted readers he provided, along with his expert counseling, helped us move forward with our academic lives.

This was before computers, when books and other printed materials had to be converted to Braille (or Brailled, as it is called) or put into large print or recorded on audiotape. This took time and had to be planned well in advance to make course materials accessible to us on the schedule needed. Volunteers would read the materials aloud to us and explain difficult subject matter to help us study for tests. I was always impressed by the dedication of these readers, who gave us three hours every weekday evening from 7 to 10 p.m. They made it possible for us to access public education at a level that made us competitive and productive. One reader, Mrs. Johnston, spent countless time audiotaping materials for me and got me through my fourth year of high school Spanish by reading and drilling me in vocabulary.

I have no idea how I got through science and math. I could not see experiments as they were conducted or geometric symbols on the chalkboard. Overzealous readers who did not want us to fail the tests they administered sometimes wrote down an answer they thought was correct, regardless of how we had answered. When I discovered this, I felt upset and insecure about my ability to succeed in a college preparatory program. Later, in college, I found a way around this by asking the reader to read me the submitted answers aloud, and insisted they change their answer to my best guess. Right or wrong, I felt better.

Other high school experiences helped build my self-esteem and social awareness. Our peers at Oakland Tech knew each other because they lived together in the local neighborhoods, while we were newly arrived and from an institution. So we had to find our way in a sighted world and a new social environment. It did not take long for us to make friends, although at first I did not feel accepted because I was not always invited to dances, parties, or gatherings of friends at the local ice cream parlor. But things began to change in two ways. In our daily study period each morning, a sighted student was designated to read assigned materials to us and also assist us in reading and answering written exam questions. These daily interactions helped us learn the basic routine of the school, and these students introduced us to others.

I was fortunate to take first year biology from Mr. Cuttitta, one of the most influential teachers I have ever had. He liked to remind us that our futures depended upon how well we approached our studies. Every so often, he would have us close our notebooks and put away the microscopes at our worktables. Then he began to speak, offering advice on how we should prepare for the future in terms of career and other life situations. I recall so clearly the words, "You will never amount to anything unless you put in a full day's work doing the best you can."

Occasionally Mr. Cuttitta would test our knowledge of the parts of a microscope. When it was my turn, I had to touch each part of the microscope and call out the name of the part. As a result, students came to know who I was and understand some aspects of my disability. Through my sophomore year, I made numerous friends just by sitting at the biology work tables with fellow students. Mr. Cuttitta went beyond his job description by empowering me to think positively about who I was and what I could become if I worked to overcome constraints, fears, and feelings of inadequacy.

After I graduated, I sent Mr. Cuttitta an annual Christmas card. To my surprise, one year when I was in college, his wife sent me a return card. She sadly reported that Mr. Cuttitta had been seriously beaten by students in his own classroom. He was out of work for quite a while. Times do change, and in my time at the school, students would never have committed such a dastardly and unforgivable act. I was fortunate to see Mr. Cuttitta one more time at Oakland Tech, in the late 1980s, when I was on a student recruitment team representing a college where I was working. I spoke with him for about ten minutes and was reminded again what a unique instructor and special person he had been to all his students.

Other outstanding Oakland Tech teachers included Mrs. Stokes, a superb Spanish instructor, Mr. Grimes, who supported my efforts in chemistry and geometry, Mr. McKay, an excellent history instructor, and Mr. Rosen, the government teacher in my senior year.

My remaining high school years were typical. I ran for class and student body offices but was unsuccessful. I had hopes of becoming a secondary school teacher and joined the Future Teachers of America club. There I gained an acute awareness of what I would need to do to prepare for college and a career in education. I was able to maintain average and above-average grades, even though I struggled with math and writing essays.

Outside the school, the world was changing rapidly, and my life changed forever on November 22, 1963, when John F. Kennedy was shot and killed in Dallas, Texas. I was sitting in fourth-period English class when someone came into the room and stated the president had been assassinated. A great silence came over the room and people began to cry. We were let out of school early that day and, as I recall, a deep sadness and depression hung over me for weeks. How could this have happened to a vivacious president and his family?

As young people, we had felt excited to witness a new, young president take on the challenges of the office and declare a New Frontier. Jack and Jackie were young and vibrant. They were art and music advocates, and reminded us that we were part of a new generation that could take us in many different directions and even to the moon. Those of course were the Camelot years, where the presidency was viewed with appreciation and respect, and where social, cultural, and creative forces came together in a vibrant atmosphere that many young people wanted to be a part of.

As President Kennedy's body lay in state in the nation's capital, an entire country was in shock. In my view, the presidency has never been the same. Lyndon Johnson was our new president, but it was as if all the air in a balloon had been let out. He could never muster up to what JFK could have achieved, even though he did a masterful job of getting Congress to pass the Civil Rights Bill in the first year of his administration. We went on living our lives, wondering what the next big event would be. After Kennedy was buried, I recall that in general people were more kind to each other. I was rehearsing to perform in the chorus of "Oklahoma" at the time. The music teacher, out of respect for that time of mourning, removed the song "Judd Fry Is Dead" because it would remind people of the assassination. The shadow of the Vietnam War was also everyday news. Many college students and minority groups were demonstrating against the war because the country's resources were financing a war instead of being directed toward housing, transportation, jobs, and education.

The Free Speech Movement at the University of California at Berkeley took center stage at the time, as students challenged archaic regulations and petitioned for the right to speak out and demonstrate for viable causes, including the disabilities rights movement headed by Ed Roberts. Roberts was a polio survivor calling attention to physical and attitudinal barriers that impeded disabled people from living normal and productive lives.

So, the public outcry and protests proved socially accurate in foreseeing, years in advance, that the United States could never win the war against the North Vietnamese, because the people in both the South and North wanted ultimately to retain their country, even under Communist control. Finally, early in 1964, the Beatles appeared on the Ed Sullivan show and launched a period of Beatlemania. I could not understand what the big craze was about—I was into Perry Como, Frank Sinatra, Andy Williams, and the Ray Conniff Orchestra.

In 1964, an election year, it appeared that Barry Goldwater, the Republican conservative, would run against Lyndon Johnson in the fall. The Republican National Convention happened to be held that July in San Francisco. Out of curiosity, one of my friends from the School for the Blind, his brother, and I, decided to attend. We each had to pay five dollars to join the Young Republicans in order to be admitted into the convention arena. We spent a few hours listening to speeches and engaging in political discussions that left us more upset than happy. Our membership did allow us to attend a convention party at the Mark Hopkins Hotel, where we sampled caviar and other delicacies. But that five dollars was my last contribution ever to the Republican Party.

Thrust into this foment of social change nationwide and in Berkeley, and with the inspiring vitality of JFK still in the air, a social movement had begun that would not disappear so quickly and would alter the social structure of the country. As part of the movement toward social activism, my fellow sighted students and I were advocates almost by default. Along with other blind and disabled people, we would soon be attending college. We were making something of ourselves and by doing so were paving the way for others to do the same.

Activism comes with the responsibility to finish what you start in spite of the odds against you. Our activism was not so much planned, but in reflecting on what has happened since then, gives evidence of what we managed to achieve. Our efforts helped bring about the Americans with Disabilities Act. Our efforts helped to improve special accommodations that allow us to compete and be a part of the social process. Our empowerment resulted from our diverse activism and the motivation to know what we could become and affirmed our presence as contributing adults in a social system that has not always been accessible to people of diversity.

Crucial to our personal and social development as residents and students at the School for the Blind was the fact that the surrounding Berkeley community accepted us. The city of Berkeley is known for its liberal politics and as home of the main campus of the University of California. Most of us at the School for the Blind, especially as we neared our high school years, had ventured out on our own or in groups to use public transportation or shop in the stores around College and Telegraph Avenues. Just a few of us used white canes, and if we needed to read a street sign, one of us with partial vision would climb up a sign pole to read the name of the street. In tenth grade, a group of us guys traveled to Candlestick Park in San Francisco to attend a Giants-Dodgers baseball game. There was no Bay Area Rapid Transit System (BART) to take us across the Bay, so we had to rely on busses and the municipal railway. We waited at various bus stops and asked fellow travelers for assistance. Everyone was helpful.

We finally reached the stadium and were escorted to our seats, where we bought some food, and turned on our transistor radios to listen to a play by play of the game. As I recall, it was spring of 1962, when the Giants beat the Cincinnati Reds and went on to become World Series finalists but lost to the New York Yankees in a seven-game playoff. Outings like this strengthened our self-esteem and our confidence that we could explore situations outside school in spite of our visual disabilities. We felt safe and comfortable in the Berkeley community. We were just young teenagers doing the things everyone else did at our age. Being disabled was not the norm, but living life to the fullest would help us prevail as individuals.

In my senior year, two special occurrences enhanced my self-esteem and social skills. A number of us guys and girls living at the School for the Blind decided to have a Friday night dance party on our campus and invite our friends from Oakland Tech. I was designated to request the approval from our school Superintendent. So, one afternoon in the spring of 1964, I ventured into Dr. Lowenfeld's office to discuss using the staff dining room for this event. He said no; this type of activity would require chaperones and create other problems. Disappointed and upset, I returned to my dorm room.

A week later, I returned to the superintendent's office with another proposal. I made the point that other teenagers were allowed to have parties and social gatherings in their homes, where parents or family members chaperoned. Since the School for the Blind was our home away from home, we should be allowed the same opportunity. Dr. Lowenfeld approved the request. At the party we enjoyed dancing, refreshments, and music. The ultimate satisfaction occurred when half a dozen of our sighted friends from Oakland Tech arrived at the party. At that moment, we felt that as visually impaired kids we had finally been accepted. Our fellow students had just given evidence that they saw us as part of their social system, not as outsiders.

The second occurrence is more personal. It was March or April when tickets for the senior ball were advertised for purchase. I had decided much earlier that I wanted to take a sighted girl to the ball and had identified who I wanted to accompany me to this special dance and afterparty. A number of us blind students advocated for total integration into the social realm of activities, and being able to go out with a sighted girl was about the greatest accomplishment a young man with a visual impairment could experience.

I wondered if I had the courage to ask Anita, a girl in my class, to the ball. Anita had always been friendly, and I had come to know her through our discussions in seventh-period reading sessions. Often, we veered off the assignment to discuss life issues or a TV show we had watched the night before. I was so nervous about asking her that I almost missed the deadline for purchasing tickets. I had consulted my friend Sheryl. "Do you think I should ask her? Do you think she might say yes? What if she says no?" My self-esteem was minimal at that point, and I was not accustomed to asking girls out to dances.

So, on Friday afternoon before the ticket closing date, I mustered the courage to ask Anita during one of our seventh-period sessions. I felt so nervous and at the same time excited. After I got the words out, she said yes. I said thank you and goodbye to her for the weekend and ran down the school hallway with a tremendous grin on my face. From that moment on, I was so happy and excited. I arranged to rent a tuxedo and buy a corsage to give her and, most essentially, bought the tickets. During the next few weeks, I could hardly concentrate on my studies.

When prom night arrived, we double-dated with another couple. Anita looked lovely in a white full-length dress. The evening was a huge success. We danced a great deal, ate good food, and talked and laughed with friends. When I dropped her off at her door that evening, we kissed each other lightly, and the evening (or early morning) came to an end. I believe I was very much in love with Anita for weeks after the senior ball. I was too inexperienced to understand what I felt, but it was probably infatuation with a beautiful girl and a wonderful person. I thank Anita for adding a great deal to my life at that time and for helping me realize I could successfully take a woman out on the town and have an enjoyable time.

Once the senior ball was over, the challenge was to pass my final exams and prepare for the graduation festivities in the Oakland Tech auditorium in June. I was excited and thrilled that I had made it through high school, and I was fortunate to receive passing grades in my major college prep courses: English, Civics, and Spanish 4. Then it was on to the graduation event. Many of us had submitted the paperwork early that would allow us to take part in the event with the ultimate prize being the presentation of our diplomas in front of family and friends.

I remember how happy my parents and grandparents were for me to attain this first major goal of my life. The celebration continued the next day with a special party at our home in San Mateo. Family and friends congratulated me, and I received many cards with money and other gifts. Afterward would be my well-earned summer vacation. Then it was time to start thinking about the next challenge, which was to start the enrollment process to attend the College of San Mateo as the first step in my post-secondary education.

Chapter 3

College of San Mateo: Challenges, Disappointments, and Successes

In the fall of 1964, the world as I knew it was changing rapidly. A movement of protests was replacing attitudes of silence where you just went along with your life, accepting the realities and explanations given to you by parents and others who had lived through depressions and wars. The Vietnam War, with U.S. involvement continuing to escalate, brought further division and countless demonstrations among young people and minorities seeking new life opportunities free from traditional values. I suddenly found myself in the new and strange environment of college life, attempting to decide if I even belonged in an environment filled with so many changes and disappointments.

It is significant to note that historically and socially people with major and visible disabilities had to continuously overcome stereotypical attitudes and social barriers that prevented them from accessing many life activities that were available to the general public. If I as a person with a disability was going to be a successful contributor to society, if my dreams of having a job and family were to materialize, I would have to jump through many barriers of ignorance, fear, and bias. In 1964, society was not yet prepared to accept disabled people as having the potential to be contributing members of society. Yes, some people with disabilities had become successful lawyers, teachers, and businesspeople, but a great deal of sacrifice, public outcry, and demonstration would need to occur in subsequent decades before the disabled population would receive the civil rights that would empower them to move forward and be a welcome part of mainstream society.

So, as I began my studies at the College of San Mateo, I was still part of what has been called the medical model of disability. Since the early nineteenth century, the notion was that if people with disabilities could be cured or fixed medically, then society would possibly invite them to be part of what was available to the general public. So, as an eager college student wanting very much to succeed in life, I felt I had no choice but to tackle whatever educational challenges were necessary to attain a college degree that could open doors for me in employment and social arenas.

In California, the Department of Rehabilitation (DOR) was the primary agency that helped people with disabilities obtain training and vocational services that would lead to degrees and certificates for placement into gainful employment. In keeping with the medical model, eligibility for DOR services depended on medical information as well as vocational and academic testing to substantiate a viable disability. So, with DOR support such as reader services, tuition support, and book vouchers, I began a long journey of adjusting to an academic culture that posed challenges enough that I would question if I could become and succeed as a college graduate.

I ascertained quickly that I would have to make sacrifices to commit to the world of studying, test-taking with readers, and planning in advance to elicit the support of Braille transcriber groups and the Recordings for the Blind organization if I wanted to climb the mountain to the ultimate outcome of a college diploma. I could not allow self-pity and depression to get in the way. (I need to emphasize that the medical model of disability did not stand alone regarding people's perceptions of disability. Social fears and stereotypes also delay integration of this diverse population. Some people carry a moral model of disability because of their negative experiences with people impacted by disability, or a religious notion that "God did this" and that a physical or mental impairment, whether driven by illness or accident, is deserved.)

It was not until 1990, when the federal government finally passed the Americans with Disabilities Act (the human rights model of disability) in response to countless demonstrations, court challenges, and social protest challenging civil rights violations, that the necessary framework was established to correct a much overdue social problem and add greater diversity to our culture and nation.

So, as the fall season approached in September of 1964, I found myself as a new student at the College of San Mateo, a two-year community college at the top of a hill overlooking the San Francisco Bay Area. I felt very nervous and extremely doubtful and wondered if I could succeed in higher education. I enrolled in four classes: English, History, Psychology, and introductory Chemistry. This course load made me a full-time student, with all the challenges and rewards of completing homework assignments, attending class lectures, and taking midterm and final exams. I had to plan ahead to hire readers, have certain materials Brailled, and schedule time with instructors to take exams in person with them in their offices. Except for history, the course materials were challenging and difficult. My stress level was high.

At the time, most college administrators and faculty, with some exceptions, questioned whether blind and other disabled students could be successful, given our many functional limitations. Yet all of us had manifested a great deal of courage and willpower to face academic challenges. It was our resolve to succeed and set an example that would make it easier for disabled students in the future to be accepted and respected. At the same time, the mid-1960s saw an influx of students at community colleges and universities. This migration caused many people in education to open their eyes to the kinds of special services that were needed for the disabled. This awareness opened doors for disabled students as more advocacy and accommodations became available for eligible disabled students to succeed in the classroom.

Academic pursuits took all my time, and social and recreational activities were put on hold for most of the semester. As the fall semester came to an end in January 1965, I took my final exams either by typing my answers on a Braille typewriter, answering test questions directly with my instructor, or having a reader review the exam with me and write my responses. I was surprised to receive one B and three Cs. With that boost of confidence, I decided to continue into the spring semester.

It became abundantly clear about one month into the semester that not only did I need to meet the many challenges of academic course work, but I would have to assert myself with some instructors so they would understand I needed special accommodations to succeed as a student. There were no regulations mandating colleges to offer such accommodations.

So, there I was, enrolled in a mandatory Western Civilization class that required us to create special projects in the form of maps depicting the location and the terrain of countries and cities in the ancient world. As a visually impaired student, I would not be able to do this assignment. The instructor was unwilling to accept my offer to work on an alternate assignment such as reading a book about Western civilization or a famous leader in the ancient world. He suggested I consider dropping his class. Upset, I took the problem to my academic counselor. He listened, then excused himself from our conversation for a few minutes. He returned to say he had just spoken with my instructor in the faculty offices, who agreed to give me the required credit if I wrote two book reports on any subject related to the course outline.

This was a special moment, and I did not recognize its significance at the time. It was the first of many conciliatory accommodations and instances of support I would receive as I progressed through my academic programs. I had won the moment by being proactive and accepting the proposed alternatives. From that point forward, my instructor was supportive, allowing me to take tests directly with him or approving my request to do a special assignment that allowed me to work at the same level as my non-disabled counterparts. At that time (1965), there were no services on campus to advocate for special accommodations for students who today meet the criteria of the Americans with Disabilities Act of 1990 and the Rehabilitation Act of 1973.

After two successful years at the College of San Mateo, I decided to continue my college endeavors at a university. After speaking with a college recruiter at the University of Santa Clara near San Jose, California, I was accepted to this small Jesuit Catholic University.

As a new student at a small university, I would quickly become aware that I was part of a community that would influence my growth as a human being. For a history major, the classes were challenging and time-consuming. I had to arrange for readers and contact professors well in advance to identify textbooks and materials, so I would be able to maintain equal footing with other students. I learned quickly that college would require me to balance my feelings of inadequacy with the determination to succeed academically and socially.

Chapter 4

Santa Clara University and the Bronco Mascot Spirit

In September of 1966, I was a new transfer student at Santa Clara University, unpacking my belongings in the brand new Swig Hall student dormitory. Ron, my first roommate, was from Monterey, California and had been a student for two years. We always ate dinner together, and he taught me how to play cribbage, which became our break from studying and writing papers. Ron assisted me at times by typing papers as I dictated and by reading me articles from current events magazines. He even served as an academic counselor, since he knew details about the courses I would need and which instructors were good or not so good. Our friendship continues to this day. Ron went on to receive a law degree from UC Berkeley and after retirement became a massage therapist. Between 2000 and 2002, Ron was my sighted guide as we completed three Big Sur marathons together.

I also became good friends with my third-year roommate, Bruce, from Hawaii. Bruce was intelligent and inquisitive and enjoyed the good things in life. We listened to classical music on my record player; we made numerous train trips to San Francisco and ate at wonderful restaurants. Bruce introduced me to cultural activities on campus and in the community that broadened my exposure and interest. Bruce, too, went on to practice law. He was a special person who took me under his wing and shaped my destiny to continue learning and enjoying concerts and fine restaurants. He also shared my interest in history and politics.

It was my good fortune at SCU to meet many exceptional people, including instructors. One of my first history classes was taught by Timothy O'Keefe, a recent graduate of St. Mary's University in Moraga, California. Tim had an abundant knowledge of European history and cared deeply about his students. He allowed me to take oral tests with him and identified in advance the books I would need to put into a recorded format for subsequent courses. I consider Tim a special friend. We don't see each other often, but when we do, we enjoy reminiscing about SCU.

History professor George Giacomoni had a tremendous influence on me. He taught U.S. History classes including diplomatic history, which I found especially interesting. His lectures made the subject came alive, and he used a range of high and low vocal tones in a way that kept my attention. He allowed me to take my test questions back to my dorm room and either Braille and then read him my answers, or type the answers and submit them directly to him. He gave me a special book on the great depression of 1929 as extra material to read in advance, so I could have more time and less stress to formulate my oral report.

At the end of my senior year at Santa Clara, I would spend two months in Europe with a tour group led by SCU instructors. George was a tour leader and I enjoyed accompanying him and rooming with him on the trip. Like Tim O'Keefe, George means a lot to me because he recognized that with the necessary accommodations I could be a successful student.

Another special instructor was Rev. Father Tennant Wright. In early 1967, I enrolled in his theology class focusing on Vatican II. Many theology issues at the time revolved around the Catholic Church, which was reforming itself to address mid-twentieth century issues that required modification to traditional values and regulations. Father Wright made me think about religion rather than just memorize facts and dates. In January or February, he would invite different Protestant ministers to the SCU mission church to celebrate their rituals alongside the Catholic traditional prayers and Eucharistic celebrations.

The Catholic church has always been a significant part of my life, and I vividly remember attending CCD (Confraternity of Christian Doctrine) classes on Saturday mornings as a child, because religious education was not available on weekdays for those of us attending public schools. I served many years as an altar boy, from age twelve, and always felt there was something special about the Mass.

As a result of Father Wright's ecumenical services, I was impressed at how much in common all the Christian church groups had. I came to realize that progressive liberal thinking was an important part of my development: It would ultimately propel me into advocating for people of diversity and for causes to correct social indifference to poverty, education, and racial bigotry.

It was also at that time that my spiritual growth began to materialize. In a fast-paced world, it was always a special time to sit in the mission church and reflect upon how I could better live my life as a Catholic Christian. The process was not to seek yes or no answers, but to reflect upon the spiritual aspects of life and attempt to find fulfillment in what I was doing. Father Wright passed away in July of 2015, leaving a legacy of kindness and good works that impacted many people here and abroad.

My ultimate success as a student at Santa Clara University depended upon specific accommodations that I either requested or were made available by necessity or common sense. At the outset, before I lived on campus, the Reverend Father John Hynes, Dean of Liberal Studies, offered his assistance and support. During the registration period prior to each quarter, he would allow me early access to my first priority classes. He arranged for a designated unoccupied dormitory room to be set aside where I could study using readers and audiotaped recordings of course materials. This support was provided without administrative protest about favoritism.

Again, there were no laws or regulations that mandated the university to accommodate my needs. This was a time of enlightenment for college administrators and faculty, as greater numbers of disabled students began attending colleges and universities across the U.S. We had to act as self-advocates and show college personnel we could excel in an integrated academic environment.

Out of these experiences I met other people whose support affected me in a positive way. I developed a lasting friendship with Charles, a fellow history student who graduated with me in 1969 and has spent his adult life practicing law. I am godfather of his oldest son, and we have maintained a wonderful relationship for over fifty years. As a student, Chuck needed a quiet place to study, and when he asked if he could use my assigned study room when I was not using it, I said "No problem." From then on, we shared many special moments and good times.

I became friends with two of my readers. Dianne always had a kind word for me and would help in any way she could. Cathleen provided reading and test support and, after our Santa Clara days, invited me to parties and other social events at her home in San Francisco. If it were not for my need of special accommodations and the willingness of Dianne and Cathleen to help me, I would not have benefitted from the friendships of these two women. Disabled people form friendships just like anyone else: it depends on where you happen to be and what you need to receive or are able to give at the time.

Santa Clara University also expanded my horizons outside classes and homework. During my three years at SCU, I sang bass in the

University chorus. Most memorable was the year we performed the Gloria, an orchestral and choral piece by Baroque composer Vivaldi. With the college chamber orchestra, we performed in the Mission Church, reminding me of how people in past centuries came together in church settings to hear and enjoy music. The University chorus frequently showcased its talents in the surrounding community.

I attended Santa Clara basketball, football, and baseball games. I once met all-star members of the San Francisco Giants at an annual exhibition game with the Santa Clara Broncos, through the help of Bob Spence, an excellent baseball player on the Santa Clara team. God must have been watching over me, because I had met Bob in a U.S. Western History class when the instructor asked if someone would be a paid reader for a visually impaired person in the class. Bob volunteered and we quickly became good friends. Prior to that exhibition game, I was invited onto the field and met famed players Willie Mays, Orlando Sapeda, Jim Davenport, and Juan Marachel. I wish I still had the baseball with all the team signatures on it. Bob and I became lifelong friends.

In my days at SCU from 1966 to 1969, two environments provided respite from the pressures I experienced as a full-time student. My dear Aunt Margie and Uncle Elton, who lived near the university, invited me to stay at their home on most weekends, where I enjoyed Auntie's pasta with authentic Italian sauce and Uncle Elton's special Manhattans. These retreats away from the academic rigors of the college environment allowed me to relax and unwind on weekends.

Another respite was the mission garden, an oasis away from the traffic of humanity wandering through their daily routines. When I became tired of my daily study demands, I often ventured out of my dorm room or the library and found a bench in the garden. As I sat among the beautiful palm trees that rose high above me, my soul became peaceful and quiet. I could hear the melodic singing of birds. If

I sat near plants and flowers, I would smell a flood of wonderful fragrances. To compensate for not being able to see details of plants and trees, I would touch the bark of a tree, move close to a flower like a red or yellow rose and experience the heavenly scent, or just sit on the bench and imagine what the garden might look like if I had normal vision. As I relaxed, my focus would turn away from my troubles and to the beauty around me. For those moments my mind was peaceful, nurturing my soul to keep moving forward. Upon exiting the garden, I would feel better about myself as I returned to the task of completing the course work I hoped would lead to a B.A. and a career job.

My self-esteem, however, was low and would continue even after I left this wonderful educational institution with its beautiful gardens and ornate buildings. In my studies, I was pleased to maintain a B average. I learned a great deal about U.S. and European diplomatic history but failed to understand many of the required philosophy and theology courses. Academic counseling was either unavailable or was provided to me by other students taking the same classes.

In retrospect, I wish I had enrolled in more psychology courses, given that a few years later I would return to Santa Clara University for postgraduate studies in the counseling psychology Master's program. In my three years at SCU, I kept asking myself if I could handle the rigors of academic coursework. The grades were there, but I felt that my knowledge and ability to retain information was inconsistent. Secondly, I spent so much time trying to keep up with my studies, that I missed out on developing social opportunities. I wondered if I would ever attract a girlfriend. I asked a young coed to attend a college event with me once, but afterward felt inadequate and self-critical.

However, looking at the other side of the coin, one of my friends was able to get me backstage to meet Ray Charles when he performed at Santa Clara University. I spoke with Ray for a few minutes and found out he had attended a school for the blind in Florida. I shared a few words about my disability, and that I had attended a similar school in Berkeley. And that was that. I went on and attended the concert and enjoyed the event. It was a unique and special moment.

A final point is that the University of Santa Clara created an opportunity to learn what I call a "vital process of life." I was able to withstand the challenges of higher education by successfully completing courses that molded into me an awareness that when I would eventually land the ultimate job, it would happen because I had gone through a rigorous process of core learning that I could apply in any job setting.

After graduation, it would be almost eight months before I would return to an educational setting. I wanted to catch my breath and do something that had nothing to do with formal education. Fortunately, several of my family members together gave me a graduation gift of a two-month tour of Europe in the summer of 1969, led by instructors from SCU. Twenty-four of us visited 18 countries in 56 days. Friendships were formed and for the most part we got along well. There were 18 women and 6 men, together night and day. My favorite countries were Austria, England, France, Ireland, Germany, Norway, Switzerland, and Spain. Most of the time the food was good, and the hotels were livable but not elegant. What I enjoyed most was visiting the Vatican, boating through the fiords of Norway, kissing the Blarney Stone in Ireland, and having crumpets and tea on a train that traveled from New Castle to London, England.

It was historic and memorable to bus from the U.S. controlled West Berlin border gate (Checkpoint Charley) into East Berlin. I was astonished at the vast difference between the two cities. West Berlin was a prosperous urban city with high-rise buildings and thriving businesses and restaurants. East Berlin showcased an austere setting with smaller buildings and vacant lots along every street. I had to laugh to myself when the East German tour guide greeted us on the bus by saying, "Welcome to the Democratic Republic of East Germany." It was a travesty for the people of East Berlin to live literally in prison every day of their lives as they looked up at the ominous brick sidings and fences of steel of the Berlin wall.

I learned a great deal from my travels in Europe in spite of some disappointments regarding my social life. As mentioned above, I had low self-esteem and had not dated much. As fate would have it, I fell for a beautiful blue-eyed blonde who I got to know rather quickly on the tour. She was friendly, attentive, and it appeared we had things in common. However, by the end of the trip, she would have little to do with me and even stood me up on a date. She had agreed to attend a musical with me and others from the group while we were in London, but when I arrived at the agreed upon location, she was nowhere to be seen. Devastated and disappointed, I attended the event, but my mind was elsewhere. However, the trip was worth it, and I learned a great deal about many wonderful places in a world outside the United States. That memorable tour was the beginning of many travel adventures I would take throughout my life, especially train travel within the U.S.

Chapter 5

Struggle and Success: Earning My Teaching Credential

As I returned home from my European travels, I began thinking about my future. I knew I wanted to work toward a secondary teaching credential, but I also wanted to find a job so I could experience the world outside an academic environment. As fate would have it, I soon found myself employed as a camp counselor at an outdoor educational summer camp for elementary school children. A friend from the School for the Blind had recommended me, and I was hired because I could read bedtime stories to children in the dark when the lights had been turned off. This was easy, of course, because I read Braille.

This was my first job, and I planned to do everything possible to perform at a high level. I hiked through the woods with the young students, planned talent shows with them, and interacted with my staff counterparts to learn specific parts of the job. During my four months at the Loma Mar Camp, near Pescadero, California, I developed a special friendship with Charlanne and Katherine, two women who would eventually introduce me to my future wife. This first job opportunity gave me the confidence to look beyond the moment and toward a career that would add financial stability and lifelong fulfillment as a full-time worker. I made only $50 a month, but at that time, earning my keep was the ultimate delight.

Even though I enjoyed the respite from academic studies, I was determined to return to the classroom to earn a secondary teaching credential. So, In January of 1970, I enrolled at the University of San Francisco and was accepted into their teaching program. I moved into the home of my paternal grandparents, Mary and Sam Dana. They were first generation Italian immigrants who had arrived in San Francisco around 1920, moving west from Illinois. They were working people who strove to learn the values and cultural morays of America without losing the ideals and life practices they brought with them from the old country.

There had always been a special love connection between Grandma Mary and me. She was not only my grandmother; she was my friend. She was a self-made woman who had taught herself how to write and speak English and made every attempt to educate herself. She did not attend college, but she managed to work in a bank, run a household, pay bills, and reach out to assist the poor and others who had less than she had. Grandma Mary was also a wonderful cook and baker. Her meals were cooked to perfection and there was always more food on the table than we could eat. I loved her spaghetti and meatballs, baked chicken, and magnificent stuffed artichokes. At birthdays and other special occasions, she ordered an Italian-rum cream cake from a North Beach bakery for dessert. It was always a feast at Grandma Mary's house. She was strong-willed, very Catholic, and always wanted to know if she could do something to help make your life a little more bearable and enjoyable. Grandma was my rock. She passed on in February of 1987, just short of her eighty-seventh birthday. Her loss left a tremendous void in my life.

So, as the new decade of the 1970s began, I had embarked on a new journey. During this period the United States was still bogged down in the Vietnam War. President Richard Nixon was determined to get us out of Vietnam by reaching out to China and the Soviet Union. His two trips to these countries opened the door for trade exchange and political interactions, a good thing for the United States. Ronald Reagan was Governor of California; John Wayne was making movies like *True Grit* and *The Green Berets,* Willie Mays was playing baseball for the San Francisco Giants, and the Dallas Cowboys were a force to be reckoned with in the NFL. On television you would find programs such as "All in the Family," "Marcus Welby," "The Fugitive," and "The Big Valley." Against this cultural backdrop, I began my class schedule at USF.

As a self-advocate, I arranged to meet with the chairman of the Education Department. We had a candid discussion, as I explained that certain accommodations would be necessary if I was going to achieve my goal of becoming a high school teacher. In 1970, there were no laws or mandates that guaranteed accommodations for students with disabilities. As we concluded our conversation, the administrator stated, with caution and concern in his voice, that I was on probation and would have one semester to prove I could be successful in the program. At that moment, I felt in my gut the pressure of the obstacles I would need to overcome and wondered if I had the ability to become a teacher. Again, I was on the front lines of the battlefield, and it was up to me to find a way to come out of this experience unblemished and with the teaching certificate I needed to move forward with my career.

Daily, I traveled by streetcar and bus from my grandparents' home on Brighton Avenue to the college at the top of the hill on Hayes Street. Ever since I was a young child, I had loved riding the streetcar. I had always felt excited when the streetcar went into the long tunnel between West Portal station and Market Street. In the tunnel, it became pitch black quickly. The speed of the car increased, the racket of the wheels on the tracks clogged my ears, and after a while I could hear only the wind noises blowing through the open windows or door panels that never closed tightly. The streetcar put me in another world free from everyday rigamarole. The biggest thrill for me was that the streetcar moved along in that massive tunnel for a long time before it came to the next stop.

In my political science course, a general education requirement, I made a dear friend. At my request, the instructor had asked in the first class session if anyone would be interested in assisting a blind student with reader support services. They would be compensated at an hourly rate by the Department of Rehabilitation for providing this service. A young man named Jay volunteered to read for me during that first semester and has been in my life ever since.

He told me later how annoyed he had been, sitting at the back of the classroom, hearing a pecking noise coming from a student sitting at the front. This distraction came from the slate and stylus I used to take notes. It was a slow process to take notes in Braille, but it was the only method available other than a tape recorder or a person who would act as a note taker and write down the lecture notes for me. I had learned early in my schooling to file down the metal tip of the stylus to reduce the sound that would call attention to me, but it was still audible. On meeting me, Jay felt embarrassed for his assumptions. Forty-seven years later, Jay and I are still best friends. He has been my rock of support and understanding. For me, Jay symbolizes all that is good in a friendship between two human beings. Jay is still my primary reader, helping me write checks and pay bills.

I soon established a routine of classes and coursework. Unfortunately, the instructor's method of providing information to students in the political issues class proved frustrating and wasted my time. The class met on alternate days, three times a week, for one hour. For each session we were required to read at least five assigned newspaper articles and be ready to answer questions about them. For me, this process was nerve-wracking. I have always had difficulty memorizing printed information quickly, without the opportunity to read and study it in advance. The news articles were not available in Braille. So, I had Jay or another reader, Cathy, who I also became good friends with and even dated a few times, meet with me in the library and read the articles to me. Even they were frustrated by the class requirement.

I should offer a bit of explanation about my learning style. I would take notes on the articles but would not be able to recall all the article contents. This is because I am not an auditory learner. I am more of a visual learner. That may sound strange, given my visual impairment, but I read Braille with my fingers, and then I recall the memory of the Braille letters in my mind, just like a sighted person might imagine an image of a paragraph or sentence they had read. I have to read an article many times with my fingers before I can remember its main points. So, for me to access information in printed form was very difficult, and half the time I felt ill prepared, frustrated, and wondering again if I belonged in a college environment.

I received a C grade in the class, and the instructor did accommodate me by allowing me to take the final exam orally in his office. But I was glad to move on to courses that I felt would better prepare me to become an effective teacher. Meeting Jay was obviously the high point of the political science class.

Although studying course materials in my two years at USF presented many challenges and disappointments, I did not realize the magnitude of change that would be required to go from being a student to being a teacher. Upon completing all of my course requirements, the time had come to complete my student teaching obligation.

I was assigned to work with Mr. Stewart, a social studies teacher at Marina Junior High School in San Francisco. Mr. Stewart was supportive and did everything he could to encourage me. In my mind, I knew my history facts and information. However, in a classroom of thirty students an instructor must be creative to maintain their attention and interest.

I quickly ascertained I was not prepared to implement creative approaches. My teacher training had focused on educational theory and the psychology of education rather than on practical ways to teach a group of students with multiple learning styles. I had spent a semester observing a master teacher, but his style was not my style. Instead of lecturing, Mr. Stewart wrote ideas or questions on the board, and asked these questions or presented the ideas to get the students involved.

I was not confident enough to use this method. My style was to have students read a chapter of material and answer my questions about it in class. I knew how to lecture to students, but I did not think about dividing them into discussion groups, or having them prepare an oral presentation, or asking them to create posters or displays for special projects. And I could have had a student volunteer to put information on the blackboard, but once it was there, and I moved on to another question or thought, I would have been unable to remember what was on the board.

I felt so disappointed in my performance that I began to think of myself as a failure. I felt I had lost the students' attention, and my confidence level went down the drain. I was always at the mercy of another person (a reader) to help me in compiling information for teaching purposes. And I did not know where to find resources and practical tools to help instructors be effective teachers.

I was assigned to teach both a U.S. history and a world history class. With each passing day, I felt more inadequate, overwhelmed, and upset with myself. Mr. Stewart suggested that I teach only the U.S. history class. The situation did not improve, and after meeting with Mr. Stewart and my adviser, we agreed I would withdraw from the program for the remainder of the semester and take summer school classes. I became very depressed and eventually sought psychiatric support. I had been teaching for only three or four weeks.

It would be months before I began to feel good about myself again. I was overwhelmed with poor self-esteem, physically and mentally drained, and still concerned that I did not belong in teaching. As the counseling sessions continued week after week, I began to identify ways to start moving out of the black clouds to a point where I could feel more positive about myself. I visited friends, took a trip or two, and ultimately decided to return to the program and obtain the teaching credential that would hopefully open job opportunities for me in the near future.

In September of 1971, about six months after withdrawing, I returned to Marina Junior High School and began for the second time to engage eighth grade students to learn something from me about U.S. history. I was fortunate to have excellent students. For the entire semester I focused on helping them understand why our Constitution is so important and teaching them about the constitutional amendments that were added to the original document due to social and historical events that mandated changes to preserve our democracy. I would spend long evenings in my room at my grandparents' house, preparing lesson plans for the next day's class.

I had no problem memorizing pertinent information to share with students, but my arsenal of teaching techniques still did not feel creative. Again, I became annoyed and frustrated with myself. I consulted with my adviser, spoke with Mr. Stewart, and kept attempting to grind through the student teaching experience. But I felt unable to teach the class in the manner I longed to do, and, for the second time, I approached coming to a complete standstill.

To escape this torturous reality, I returned home at the end of each school day and went to bed, an escape that provided minimal solace. My concerned grandparents called my Aunt Margaret, who worked in San Francisco at the time. She was my godmother and loved me very much. She was just the person to kick me out of bed, figuratively if not literally.

Aunt Margie, or Auntie, as we called her, had been raised in the Depression years and was greatly influenced by her parents to work hard, study consistently in school, and adhere to parental demands without question. Grandma Mary had taught Margaret how to manage a household and how to make your hard-earned money go as far as possible. Auntie attended business school and went to work at a young age. As far back as I can remember, Aunt Margie had nurtured and supported me through good times and struggles. She had introduced me to classical music, great movies, and wonderful restaurants. Her second marriage would last for almost four decades. Neither of my grandparents drove a car, and Aunt Margie took them shopping. Auntie was a major force in my life. She showed up at my grandparents' house the day they called and spent a good hour giving me love and hell in her loud, assertive voice for not finishing what I had started. She was attempting to motivate me to get on with my life. I had to quickly decide what I was going to do.

Somehow I managed to hang in and taught the rest of the class. I received a good report from my master teacher, and in January of 1972 completed the student teacher program and received the coveted teaching credential.

What I did not realize was that I had made a positive impression on my students. On my last day as their student teacher, they presented me with a gift and thank you card. That I had stuck it out and did so as a partially blind individual had gotten their attention.

It is my firm belief that everyone who is constantly troubled by emotional and mental issues should seek a professional counselor or psychotherapist who can objectively listen and help them begin the long process of healing. Throughout my life, I have found both prayer and therapeutic counseling to be wonderful resources as I struggled with unexpected life challenges. I believe that my effectiveness as a counseling professional—which was my ultimate direction—was greatly enhanced by my experiences as a recipient of such supportive services.

Chapter 6

Entering the World of Work: Finding the Right First Job

I was not sure what I would do next, but I knew there was a place for me in the world of work if I could maintain my optimism. I traveled around California visiting family and friends. I went to Monterey and stayed with Ron, my friend and roommate from USC, who had just returned from the Peace Corps and was headed to Bolt Hall in Berkeley to study law.

Another person I spent time with was my second cousin Sylvia. In the early 1950s, Sylvia had contracted polio and became severely disabled. She survived over fifty surgeries, acquired a master's degree in social work, and for many years worked for the Department of Social Services in her hometown of Santa Rosa. I had visited Sylvia often. She helped me recognize that my limitations as a visually impaired person should never impede my efforts to live a constructive and meaningful life. Sylvia was articulate and passionate about the need for disabled people to develop a feeling of empowerment. She promoted psychotherapy and counseling as resources for finding a way through the maze of life and for attaining the balance to endure mental and physical challenges. She gave me some tough love: I could do more with my life than feel sorry for myself.

I was always struck by Sylvia's determination and exuberance. She drove a small four-door Oldsmobile sedan with modified hand and foot controls. Later in her life, as she succumbed further to Post-Polio Syndrome, she purchased a large SUV that had a lift for her to enter and exit the vehicle. She drove to work every day on her own, went shopping on her own, and visited friends and family by driving around in her modified and high tech vehicles.

One day Sylvia and I were driving in her Oldsmobile on an old country road in Lake County. Something went wrong with the car, and she pulled over. It turned out we had a flat tire. Immediately, memory of a recent argument with my father surfaced. I had asked him to show me how to change a flat tire. He had refused. He was concerned that the jack would slip and severely injure my hands or fingers, in which case I would be unable to read Braille, which was essential in my studies and future profession. I became upset and argued with him. I had witnessed some of my totally blind friends fix flat tires. My argument went nowhere. When I was younger, my dad had been excited and proud watching me wrestle sighted opponents at the School for the Blind. He was proud when, on a vacation trip, he happened to observe what a good swimmer I had become, and my few laps doing the crawl stroke impressed him. But he was disappointed that his first son had been born visually impaired, and I've been told he was not the same after my birth. His disappointment, concern, and frustration pointed to his preconceived notions about disability issues and what I could and could not handle.

In the car with Sylvia, I was annoyed that I would be handling this mild emergency by the seat of my pants. "Thanks, Dad," I said sarcastically to myself.

So, there we were, a severely disabled woman and a visually impaired young man, faced with removing a flat tire and replacing it with a spare. Together, we got the jack in place and removed the tire. Everything went well. I managed not to injure myself or Sylvia and tightened the cogs of the spare tire as securely as I could.

When we arrived back at Sylvia's home, her father, a mechanic, informed me that I had completed this major task correctly, except I had put the tire bolts on backward. We had still made it to our destination, and I was pleased that I had been able to help Sylvia.

After that, I practiced using the car jack and taking tires off their rims with a wrench and bolt tool. I felt prepared enough that in a similar emergency, I could help my future wife or kids or someone else. I understand where my father was coming from, but at the time I wanted him to accept the possibility that with proper training I could fix a flat tire.

A job turned up soon after I'd done a bit of traveling to see friends. I had applied for Department of Rehabilitation services many years before, in hopes I would be placed into gainful employment. In April of 1972, I received a phone call from my Rehab counselor, Jack Brazil, asking if I was interested in coordinating a summer program to help visually impaired high school graduates make the transition to college at the University of California at Santa Cruz. I said yes immediately.

I packed my bags and traveled to Santa Cruz and immersed myself in learning all I could about the program. I was given an office and lived in the college dorm with the twenty or so program participants. My job was to provide counseling to the students, ensure they had reader support, and arrange for weekly seminars featuring blind and sighted guest speakers on the subject of how to transition to college. Most of the time, I had to make decisions and arrange activities without knowing the full scope of the program mission.

I had minimal knowledge of how to run a program. I relied upon my instincts, my college training, and my own experience as a visually impaired student. I ran workshops and invited speakers to talk to the group about social and political issues related to blindness. I learned by doing.

I was able to interact with all my students and share my personal experiences. I emphasized the need to take the initiative and be creative in educating their instructors about the need for getting books recorded in advance, finding readers, and making test-taking arrangements. At the end of the six-week program, I realized I could successfully perform a job in a setting that nurtured students. I also felt certain my current and future success depended upon having a positive attitude and making every effort to prepare myself for obstacles that might arise. College had given me the advantage of an education, but it would take time to learn how to apply that knowledge and refine my skills in a work environment. At the end of the program, I was pleased to receive a check for a thousand dollars, the most money I had ever made. I felt excited and optimistic because I had successfully run a summer program.

Immediately after the job ended, I was hired by the California Department of Rehabilitation in San Jose as a full-time assistant rehabilitation counselor. I confess I had some help. My father had approached a good friend who knew Michael Deaver, a top assistant to Governor Ronald Reagan. That friend sent a letter of recommendation to Mr. Deaver, which was forwarded to state agency administrators at the local level. The next thing I knew, my rehab counselor phoned to tell me I was being considered for a low-level rehabilitation aid position. After an interview with a panel of DOR staff, I began my nine-year tenure with this state agency.

My primary job responsibility was to provide homemaker support services to recently blinded people who needed special services to make the transition to living with a visual impairment. Even though this job came through the influence of a friend, I took nothing for granted. I would spend the next nine years providing rehab program assistance to diverse clients who wanted to move on with their lives but needed independent living services such as counseling, mobility training, Braille training, special visual aids and cooking resources, and whatever else was required to sustain independent living.

It took me a number of years to fully understand the rehabilitation services model. But as my knowledge and experience built, I became an increasingly effective advocate for my clients. I visited people in their homes, offering support, hope, and practical strategies that would help them live normal lives. I often referred clients to other special programs for the blind and visually impaired.

Many of my clients attended the Orientation Center for the Blind in Albany, California. There they lived on the campus for four to six months and learned the skills of daily living (such as cooking, travel, and mobility) much more quickly than if I'd visited them once a week at their homes. Whether my clients received services at home or in another program, the bottom line for me was to begin the steps necessary for these individuals to be rehabilitated not just in the skills of daily living, but also on a path toward employment if possible. Employment was part of the Department of Rehabilitation's mission.

I did not know at the time that my nine-year tenure at the DOR was building a foundation that would empower me throughout my professional career. The Department of Rehabilitation was and still is a nationwide program that offers eligible people with disabilities the opportunity to train and prepare for gainful employment. Clients of DOR must have a classified disability, a specific job-related disability, and a strong likelihood that rehab support will help them overcome barriers to employment. It was my job to assess a client's eligibility and develop a rehabilitation plan outlining services and resources they would need to accomplish their objectives. I learned the Department of Rehabilitation process from the ground up.

I learned to cope with both personnel and client issues. In meetings, listening to dialogue between my counterparts and the supervisor awakened me to the reality that I knew very little about being a rehabilitation counselor and about the many procedures available to assist clientele. I made a consistent effort to keep my ears and eyes open. I was provided a program secretary who was available to read materials aloud to me and type up case notes I had dictated. DOR provided a driver to take me to client appointments and community service agencies. These special accommodations were crucial for my success. Had I been employed in the private sector at that time, there was no Americans with Disabilities Act (ADA) that required employers to provide accommodations for employees with disabilities.

As time passed, it became apparent to me that something was amiss about my job. My counterparts were advancing to new positions and I was remaining as a rehabilitation counselor/teacher for the blind. My goal was to become a generalist counselor who provided services to the general population of people with disabilities, not just the blind. However, as far as management was concerned, I could have stayed in my current position for the remainder of my working career. The agency preferred to keep visually impaired employees working on blind services caseloads instead of encouraging them to move on to positions with greater opportunities for advancement.

A little over a year after I began the job, I applied to take the written and oral exams for a rehab counselor position and was accepted. I moved up from the assistant counselor position I had been working in.

I encountered some special people at the DOR during those spirited days in the San Jose area. I was impressed with the wonderful secretarial support I received from the women who worked in the district office. They went beyond the call of duty to make sure my files were up to date and that I was current on departmental memos circulated in the office. I regarded all of them as friends, who in their own way were looking out for me and were determined to help me succeed as a novice employee. Certain coworkers always took time out to listen to my concerns and make wonderful suggestions as to how I might assist my clients. Their support taught me a great deal about how other professionals could work out issues and solve complex problems related to client matters and agency bottlenecks. I became close friends with Bonnie, who drove me to work every morning and included me in her social life and later in her family when she was married.

Early in my work at DOR I met John Crane, who worked for Goodwill Industries in San Jose. We met at a conference hosted by the American Association of Workers for the Blind. John sat at my lunch table and began talking to me. I quickly realized he was a special person. He had been a hospital equipment salesperson, and one tragic day in San Francisco, stepped off a curb and was hit by a car. After months in the hospital, followed by a long rehabilitation period, he landed a job with Goodwill Industries. He lived in constant pain, and his employment options were limited. But he made the best of things and graciously helped and supported many people with physical and mental impairments. John was my father's age, and he was always there to make life feel special for me. Over the years we had ongoing discussions about our lives and how we could best meet our challenges. We laughed and cried together, and we met each other's families.

Certain clients also stand out. Many of these folks had recently succumbed to blindness as a result of an accident or eye disease. In my view, these rehabilitation clients (along with disabled students I would eventually assist later as a college academic counselor) are unsung heroes who applied their own hearts and souls to overcome adversity brought about by mental and physical disabilities. A substantial number of these people fought tooth and nail to live their own lives without any support services. My initial thought about some of them was, how on earth can I help a person who is not motivated to modify their life to adapt to living with a new or unexpected disability? Each time, I rolled up my sleeves and dove into the job with an open mind and the initiative to work through as many of the problems as possible.

Individuals I had marginal success with saddened me because they gave up their struggle or just decided to live out their lives in despair. One young man had great potential as a computer technology professional but would not listen to suggestions about his dietary and physical conditioning. He was diabetic and continuously ate and drank in a way that impaired his health. Another client had partial vision due to a condition known as albinism. He was kindhearted but unwilling to give up driving a car. He was arrested often for driving without a license and consequently never completed his rehabilitation program.

Among the success stories, three people come to mind. Joan was a wonderful, kind person who worked through many personal problems and reactions to blindness. She too was a diabetic faced with making many lifestyle adjustments. She attended the Orientation Center for the Blind, and when she came home, lived a normal life helping others adapt to their disabilities. Joan passed away many years ago, but I will always remember her optimism and attitude of sharing herself with others. I miss her very much and like to imagine her in heaven, lending support and grace to people who need a special lift in their afterlife.

My challenge as a rehab counselor was put to the test when I met Laura. She had lost all her vision due to Diabetic Retinopathy. Up until then, Laura had lived a very active life and was a schoolteacher. When I met her, she was depressed, confused, and dominated by her parents' reluctance to let her live independently. She felt she had nowhere to turn to help her live a productive life without being able to see. I spent a good two years helping Laura. At first, I spent many hours just letting her vent, and occasionally suggested some options to help her start on the road to a normal life.

At the time, I had just started a graduate program in counseling psychology at Santa Clara University, so I was developing my counseling skills. As I became more familiar with Laura's issues, I incorporated my new knowledge as I sat with her in her living room. One important axiom of being an effective counselor is to allow your clients or students to bond with you so that they feel confident and trusting as they share parts of themselves with you. Some of these tools include unconditional positive regard, reflecting back to clients what they have just said, asking what, how, and why questions, maintaining objectivity, and always being nonjudgmental. Laura's predicament was that she had lost her self-confidence, and because she was with her parents, was continuously being treated as a visually impaired person who would need help to live independently.

One fine summer day, I finally broke through Laura's fears and concerns to the point where she agreed to attend the Orientation Center for the Blind. It was a crucial moment. If she was not going to take this step forward, I had no option but to terminate rehab services. Laura agreed to tackle the new challenges, and the rest is history. At the center she learned how to read Braille, prepare and cook meals, and master mobility obstacles by learning orientation skills in both her home and external environments.

Subsequently, she was accepted in the computer training program at the Center for Independent Living in Berkeley. Approximately a year later, Laura completed her degree work, was hired at a big technology company, and has been employed ever since. Laura will always be special to me and I am grateful I had something within me to help her attain the awareness that moved her toward a productive lifestyle.

Finally, there was Doug, one of my first clients in 1973. He lived in San Jose with his young wife and daughter and had lost his vision due to diabetes. Before that, he was a postal worker and was also adept at woodworking. One night I was invited to his house for dinner. I looked forward to an enjoyable evening with Doug and his family. (Occasionally, I took off my rehabilitation hat and replaced it with my social, friendly-neighbor sombrero.) As we sat down to the dinner table, Doug's wife served him a piece of chicken and, without a word, he lobbed the piece of meat back at his wife.

I am unable to share details, but clearly Doug was depressed and angry about his life situation. He was still in the grieving process and could not accept the reality of total blindness. It took many counseling sessions and much prodding to get Doug to attend the Orientation Center. He spent six to eight months there and vastly improved his attitude. Given that he would never be able to return to work, his wish was to be able to carry on with his many woodworking projects. He requested that DOR buy him an electric saw and other tools to make wood products that he could use or give away as gifts. It took me a while to convince my supervisor to approve this request, because he had doubts Doug could benefit from this expensive tool. My argument was that DOR had purchased sewing machines for blind female clients. We would be doing a similar thing for Doug to enhance his independent living options.

Doug spent the remainder of his life creating beautiful wood products, including a wooden rolling pin I still have today. I was so pleased that Doug found a niche and that because of our persistent help and support, his quality of life was enhanced. In late 1979 Doug passed away from an unexpected heart attack. All who knew him were devastated. I will never forget Doug and what he stood for. His kind and giving nature along with his wonderful wife and daughter will always have a place in my heart.

These three stories are a very small sample of what I experienced in my formative years as a rehabilitation counselor. These and other experiences during my tenure in San Jose gave me a sense of purpose to keep moving forward and pursue other career avenues that would let me apply what I had learned to new situations and to do good works for those I served as a public employee.

Chapter 7

Married Life and a Family

Back in the summer of 1969, when I was working as a camp counselor in Pescadero, I had become good friends with two women who worked at the camp—Charlanne, a naturalist, and her mother, Catherine, one of the cooks. Charlanne often mentioned her cousin Eileen, who lived in New York. She wanted me to write to Eileen. She thought we might become good friends, or more.

It was not until 1975, after ending a discouraging relationship, that I followed through on Charlanne's suggestion. Eileen and I began a casual correspondence about our interests—family and friends, politics, religion, and the like. We would occasionally speak by phone, and I was always impressed by her sweet voice and her New York accent.

As the year moved into 1976, I decided to open up avenues to enhance my social life and broaden my career options by enrolling in graduate school to earn a Master's degree in Counseling Psychology at the University of Santa Clara. I soon grew busy with night classes.

The year 1976 was full of bicentennial celebrations. America was occupied with paying tribute to our forefathers and declaring our positive attributes as a nation. Washington D.C. showcased concerts, military expositions, and plenty of fireworks. Church bells were rung, cannons fired, and ship bells and horns continuously heard on internal rivers and bays and sea outlets. For moviegoers, theaters were showing *Network, Rocky, The Shootist,* and *The Enforcer.* "Rich Man Poor Man" was the most watched TV series of the year. If you wanted fast food and went to McDonalds, a Big Mac, fries, and a drink would cost you close to one dollar. If you walked around North Beach in San Francisco looking for an authentic Italian restaurant, the menu in the window at Flower of Italy Restaurant offered a three-course meal for about ten dollars. Jimmy Carter, Governor of Georgia, ran against Gerald Ford for the U.S. presidency and won. And in October, the fall baseball classic had the Cincinnati Reds sweeping the New York Yankees four games to zero.

In my job at the DOR, I had been accepted into a special training program for rehab counselors that would take place at the Helen Keller Center for the Deaf/Blind in Sands Point, New York, in March. I had two weeks' vacation on the books and traveled to Texas to visit cousins before the trip. I also arranged to meet and spend two days with Eileen Redmond at her home in Syracuse.

In New York, the friend who drove me from Sands Point to Grand Central Station was late, and I almost missed the train to Syracuse. I was just in time to grab my luggage and get aboard. I was nervous and wondered if I should turn around and fly back to California. I had no idea what Eileen looked like or what she would be like in person. It didn't cross my mind that she was probably having similar thoughts about me.

The letters I'd received from Eileen had offered me hope she might be interested in me. We had mutual interests in family, religion, hiking, and sports, and my blindness made no difference to her. She was a nurse, so both of us were in the helping professions. Eileen was raised a Catholic and had attended parochial schools in Syracuse. I was down and out at the time, and I guess I had put my hopes in Eileen.

Eileen picked me up at the Syracuse train station on a spring day in March and drove me to the apartment she shared with her father and sister. They invited me to dinner and afterward she and I took an evening walk around the neighborhood. The next day, on a tour of the area, we visited a park with many trails and came across a big black snake alongside the path. It scared the hell out of us, but the snake didn't move, and I took Eileen's hand and led us around it with no problem. I noticed how soft her skin felt against my hand. We had lunch at the popular Hyde's Hot Dogs restaurant and dinner again at her apartment. I flew back to San Jose that evening.

That visit in March changed my life. Right away, I was attracted to Eileen. She was kind, I loved her laugh, and she had a warm personality. I was taken by her long brown hair, her smile, and her wonderful attitude about things. I was not able to see her blue eyes, but I could see her smile. I thought she was one of the most beautiful women I had ever seen. We were about the same height. The attraction was mutual. I knew right away that I loved her, and Eileen told me later that she probably had decided then and there she was going to marry me.

We continued writing and spoke often by phone for the next three months. In July, Eileen moved to Pescadero and stayed with her aunt, and three weeks later moved in with me at my apartment in Santa Clara. We were married on October 9, 1976. It was a small family affair and the happiest day I had ever experienced.

Settling into married life was both challenging and wonderful. Our love for one another grew with each passing day. Of course, we had arguments and disagreements. The difficult thing in any relationship is to learn how to give more than you think you can and let things go that in the long run have little significance.

Eileen had worked in geriatrics nursing, and she applied right away for a California license. Our immediate goal was to save money for a down payment on a house. Our first home was in Hayward, in the East Bay, where we lived for four years until I left the DOR to take a new job in Sacramento.

I will always remember our time in Hayward because I became a father. Monica Elisabeth Dana was born on August 5, 1978. When Monica was put into my arms for the first time, I felt excitement and an immediate love connection that created a strong and enduring bond between us.

In fact, Monica was the first child to be born into the Dana family since 1953, when my sister Marianne arrived in the world. It is always an adjustment for both parents when a new child is born into the family. Prior to Monica's birth, I felt both excited and uncertain about bringing a child into the world. I wondered if I could be a good father and feared that a new baby would in some way change my relationship with my wife. Of course, none of these trepidations materialized. The reality of childbirth and greeting a daughter was more than enough to overcome my fears.

Eileen's sister Terry moved to San Francisco in the summer of 1978, just after Monica's birth. Like Eileen and their sister Maureen, she worked in the nursing profession and spent many years working at the Sisters of the Poor nursing home in San Francisco. As our family grew, we spent summers and holidays with Terry in San Francisco. Terry is full of the Redmond family spirit, and has made a difference in all of our lives as we continue to receive special gifts from her goodwill and kindness.

A year and a half later, in January of 1980, Carolyn Marie Dana would come into this world, full of life and vigor. In 1981, two days after Thanksgiving and two months after we moved from Hayward to Sacramento for my new job, Jennifer Lynn Dana was born. We would eventually have two more children—Laura Ann in July 1985 and Michael Thomas in December 1990. I never thought I would be the father of five children, but with each baby a special bond occurs between child and parent. I was present for the birth of each child. The ability to love and nurture our children is an opportunity I have always welcomed and cherished. Every child has its own personality, and it made me proud to witness their progress in life and to be there to comfort them during disappointments and hard times. I have enjoyed the responsibilities of fatherhood, even though at times my children's lives were challenged with disappointments and sadness. The rhythm of the peaks and valleys of life sustains us, no matter how difficult it is to deal with them.

Michael to this day astonishes me with his good humor and easygoing attitude about life. He has developed skills in organic farming and the preservation of the environment. His willingness to take on hard work and his goodwill to others are signs he will be successful at whatever he does. Michael and I have always been very close. We have attended baseball games together, hiked outdoors, and shared many memorable moments in conversations and joking around. My relationship with Michael seems to get better as we age.

Years ago, I christened my youngest daughter, Laura, with the nickname "Sweets" because of her loving and happy disposition, even as a child. Laura did well in school and completed a four-year degree program in hotel management and culinary arts. She is a consultant in the hotel and restaurant business and highly respected by her peers. As with Michael, Laura and I have developed a special bond and can share our thoughts and concerns with openness and respect for each other. We settle misunderstandings quickly. I love spending time with Laura. She will always be a bright light in my life because of who she is and her gifts of sincere love and kindness that, to me, are beyond description.

One day as I sat at my computer writing this book, I called Monica on my cell phone to congratulate her on turning forty. Because Monica was the first child and first girl in the Dana family since my sister Marianne, she received a lot of attention in the family. Monica has fine taste and always looks spectacular when she goes out. Despite some struggles with work and relationships, Monica has a tremendous amount of determination and courage. She never married but has a son, Donovan, who has grown into an outstanding young man. It is gratifying to me that Monica has learned to handle her struggles in a constructive way. I have watched her earn a college degree, take many steps to live a productive and satisfying life, and gain self-esteem as she moves into older adulthood. I am proud of her and vividly recall our special moments.

As a young girl, Monica would accompany me on bike rides through the neighborhoods we lived in. I should not ride a bike because of my poor visual acuity, but with Monica I would ride slowly and take no chances. She would ride just ahead or side by side with me, depending on whether we were riding on the sidewalk or a side street with little traffic. We usually rode to a nearby park where she played on the swings and slides. Maybe we'd stop for an ice cream cone as well. Monica enjoys a full and active life, and when I tag along with her now from time to time, I never know what kind of surprise I will experience. We have an annual tradition of attending Giants games in San Francisco. All my children are San Francisco Giants fans like their dad.

Carolyn, our second child, died in an automobile accident on October 9, 2011, on our thirty-fifth wedding anniversary. Carolyn was a special young lady, intelligent and beautiful, and she enjoyed swimming and being with friends. She and Monica were always close. I always thought Carolyn lacked self-esteem, and as she grew into adulthood this became more apparent as she faced challenges that at times overwhelmed her. In her thirties her relationship with her partner deteriorated, and she suffered from depression. At that point, Carolyn seemed to me a lost soul. She was a very loving person and a good mother to her two children. But her self-esteem issues and inability to deal with life's struggles culminated in a downhill slide that led her into despair and the eventual accident that ended her life. I often ask myself what her life would have been like had she dealt with her problems more constructively. I believe she would have found a career she enjoyed and married someone who loved her deeply and helped fill the deep gap in her life to free her from despair and dysfunction. When Carolyn was a child, a friend used to call her Miss America because of her inner and outer beauty. When she was a little girl, she would always come and sit beside me on the stairway leading to the second floor of the house. As an adult, she told me once, "I did that because I wanted to be near you because I loved you so much." Eileen and I assumed full-time guardianship of her two sons, Cullen and Keegan. Carolyn will always be close to my heart.

My third daughter, Jennifer Lynn, has been married for over ten years. Her three beautiful daughters make me proud to be their grandfather. Jenny is assertive and opinionated on just about any subject, and though we don't always agree, especially about politics and religion, we always resolve our differences quickly and go on loving one another. She has always been proactive, with a strong determination to be a success at whatever she decides to do. She always has an eye out to help and support people, whether they are friends, family, or those she does not know. Jenny works for a state health department and is very busy being a mother and wife and assuming other roles outside the family. I always feel proud of Jenny, despite her stubbornness. She is genuine in everything she does.

In my view, the family is the primary foundation of our lives. Our family interactions and experiences mold us into the people we become. We are nurtured, supported, loved, and disciplined by those around us who influence our very existence.

Chapter 8

Sacramento: The Rollercoaster Years

As a new father, I was always thinking about the future. By my sixth year at the DOR in San Jose, I knew everything I needed to successfully perform my job as a rehab counselor for the blind. I believed I had the ability to progress further, given my experience as a counselor and my recent Master's degree. I needed a change in venue, with the hope of earning more income.

I had also developed a growing awareness that there were few opportunities for promotion within the DOR. Counselors who had a physical or mental disability were often overlooked when transfer or promotion opportunities became available. Some people who were blind and disabled did move up the ladder, but not many. This was likely an unconscious bias on the part of the administrators. There was no ADA yet, and this bias could have stemmed from administrators' own negative experiences in dealing with people of diversity including those with disabilities.

Through friends and professional acquaintances, I applied for a lateral job transfer to the California State Personnel Board in Sacramento, California. When I received the offer to work there as a Staff Services Analyst, I jumped at the opportunity. I would become a statewide recruiter to encourage people of diversity including women, minorities, and persons with disabilities, to apply for state positions through the required examination process. So, in September of 1981, after nine years at the DOR, I moved to Sacramento with my growing family to begin the second chapter of my career journey.

Late that month, I walked into a new department, a new office, and a new job that would require me to learn skills related to analytical staff work. The transition was difficult. I had no idea how I would be able to look at a data sheet full of statistics and prepare a written report about them. It took almost six months before I grasped the significance of how accepted applications for state employment could impact Affirmative Action requirements. I also had to learn how to present information to diverse community groups about the merits of State service. The job also involved heading Qualified Appraisal Panels to interview qualified job applicants and assign them a ranking on the employment list. As the panel chairperson, I had to make sure every candidate got a fair shake.

State employment is based upon applicants completing written tests and oral interviews. My job was to develop a recruitment plan that would ensure qualified individuals would properly complete the application so they could move forward in the various employment stages. We had to follow state and federal Affirmative Action guidelines to ensure that women, the disabled, and people of different nationalities would be informed and targeted for the employment exams.

I arranged for newspaper ads to appear throughout the state and scheduled outreach recruitment activities such as public meetings and orientation seminars. I made numerous presentations teaching applicants how to tackle the state bureaucracy in order to apply and compete effectively for jobs. I enjoyed making presentations and providing people with information and resources to help them find jobs. I walked people through the process for filling out the job application correctly. I talked about the employment list they would be placed on after their test or panel interview. I told them the number of hires in specific departments and sometimes invited a state employee to speak about their experience in a specific department. The final phase in this process was preparing a report showing the percentage of applications that were accepted for further consideration in each target group, to indicate if the numbers met mandated Affirmative Action standards.

After about two years in this position, I wanted to be promoted into an Associate Personnel Analyst position. The job required an oral exam that entailed much study and preparation. I took the exam twice and eventually received a passing score, almost four years after I started the process. During this period, I also realized I did not want to remain in a job that required me to interpret data and write reports analyzing this material. I had the ability to do the work, but my heart was elsewhere. My calling was to be a counselor or teacher, not a data analyst.

This situation came to a head sometime in 1984 or '85 when I had obtained a job transfer to the Department of Motor Vehicles headquarters and worked in the Equal Employment Opportunity (EEO) division. Our mandate was to process EEO complaints. I learned to evaluate discrimination complaints, make reports, and monitor these cases through the complaint process. I enjoyed being available for employees in this process. I excelled at this role because it drew on the counseling skills I had learned at the Department of Rehab and the knowledge I'd gained in graduate school.

However, the DMV was a very different environment from the Personnel Board. At times, when the workload was light or without a pressing deadline, some managers would assign work that made no sense. My frustration intensified when I had to write reports and modify publications that required much more than minor alterations. My supervisor was a career administrator and political appointee who showed no mercy when it came to wanting things done her way. At one point, she asked me to rewrite a large procedures manual. With only a part-time reader to help me, the assignment was impossible. I told the supervisor I could not do this. Her response was to have me transferred back to the Personnel Board for not passing my probationary period.

So, once again, I wanted to find a job that would allow me to use my skills to support individuals with special challenges and needs. In the meantime, however, I had to carry on and do the best I could. Part of the employment challenge is to hang in there, take your lumps, and try to build upon adversity by finding positive aspects in the experience. I did just that, and in future positions I would discover that my success was due in part to the analytical work experience I had at the DMV and State Personnel Board. As a Staff Analyst, I had become a more effective and organized writer. These vital communication skills enabled and empowered me to be an effective academic counselor and coordinator of disabled student services at various community colleges where I would eventually work.

As I mulled over what current and future employment options might be available to me, life continued outside work. The biggest personal challenge in our life in Sacramento was the neighborhood we lived in. The real estate agent had not told us much about the location. And although Eileen and I had slight reservations about buying the house, they were not significant enough that we'd shared them even with each other. As it turned out, cars would speed down the street, we were robbed twice, and the house next store was torched, threatening our home.

Nevertheless, we experienced special family moments that enhanced our lives. During our years in Sacramento, from 1981 to 1985, my oldest girls started attending school and made some good friends. Eileen also developed friends and was working part time as a nurse, including every other weekend, during which I would take care of my two young daughters. After our third daughter, Jennifer Lynn, was born in 1981, Eileen stopped working. During the summer, we took trips to Lake Tahoe, Santa Cruz, and San Francisco. Our fourth daughter, Laura Ann, was born in mid-1985. We had a swing set in the back yard and I fondly remember sitting in a small wading pool with my daughters playing water games and trying to stay cool in the hot Sacramento summers. I started running as well, and joined the local Toastmasters organization, which empowered me to speak with confidence to small and large groups of people on the job. I met people who are still in my life, especially my friend Rick, from the DMV, with whom I ran several 5 and 10K races, and our families socialized together.

Even though I lived and worked in Sacramento for only five years, I accomplished a great deal in my career during this period and developed lifelong friendships.

Chapter 9

A New Career Direction

It was late 1985 when Eileen spotted an ad in local magazine for a Disabled Students Programs & Services (DSPS) Coordinator position at a small community college in northern California. As luck or misfortune would have it, I submitted an application and was immediately invited for an interview. To prepare, I contacted DSPS coordinators at other California colleges to ask about the nature of their jobs and the college environment. Eileen drove me to this small community in the mountains for the interview. Four weeks later I was offered the job.

I was excited to transition from state civil service into the community college system, because I knew from the bottom of my heart that I was meant to work directly with disabled students to help them take advantage of secondary education opportunities.

On a cold rainy day in early January, my buddy Jay drove me in a pickup truck from my home in Sacramento to a cottage in the town where I would live for the first semester, prior to my family joining me. The temperature was at or below freezing, and snow covered the surrounding mountains. Jay helped me move my belongings—a few pieces of furniture including a TV—into the cottage, which was bitter cold because the heat would not be turned on without an additional rental fee, which I would not have for two weeks. We did manage to find a small propane heater from the secretary of the Disabled Student Services program, who happened to live in the neighborhood, that I could use for those two weeks. My father eventually brought me a carpet that helped to make the place more bearable in the winter months.

Jay dropped me off the next morning at my new office, about a mile away on the college campus, where I stepped into an adventure that would allow me to work in a challenging academic and counseling position, but with complicated issues and heartbreaks that would change my life and at the same time strengthen my resolve and fortitude to overcome adverse circumstances.

When I was introduced to the college and staff, I immediately felt I was in a good place to meet new people, share confidences and information with colleagues, and above all use my skills and talents to help students with their academic and vocational needs. My first challenge was to familiarize myself with the Disabled Student Services program policies and regulations. As counselor/coordinator of the program, my responsibility was not only to serve students but also to direct full- and part-time staff, ultimately eight or so people.

I also had to acquaint myself with the California community college educational requirements for students pursuing degrees. I quickly began the long and difficult process to guide students through their course decisions and support their progress while ensuring that they received the individual accommodations that would reduce social and educational barriers. I understood what visually impaired students needed, but when it came to students with learning disabilities, I had to follow recommendations from the learning disability (LD) specialist who administered specialized testing to determine how to best meet those needs. I also had to learn to manage program budgets.

In general, the college faculty and staff supported the DSPS program and my efforts. I still doubted that I had the knowledge and ability to succeed at the job, even though it was what I had wanted to do. It required a mental vigilance to remind myself to stop thinking such nonsense and focus on the tasks at hand.

As time went on, I grew more confident and was proactive in attending training conferences and establishing community liaisons. I attended my first annual conference of the California Association for Post-Secondary Education and Disability (CAPED), an association of disabled and nondisabled professionals. At the four-day event I met colleagues from other community and state colleges and universities, and was excited to learn from colleagues and witness the vast and profound expertise in the group.

The most interesting workshop I had ever experienced was led by Dr. Paul Longmore, a brilliant history professor from San Francisco State who lived a full and productive life as a person with cerebral palsy. His stories about the history of cultural attitudes toward people with disabilities were fascinating. In some parts of the world, he pointed out, people believe God or another deity causes a child to be born with a physical disability, and others should keep away from such persons to avoid "catching" their disease. Even today, in some communities in the western world, parents tend to keep their disabled children at home out of shame and fear they won't be able to take on the challenges of life.

I began to study this topic and incorporated historical and cultural references on disability into my presentations and workshops. Within CAPED I became a chairperson for counseling and employment professionals. As CAPED members, we were encouraged to join groups to present and exchange information as well as brainstorm on pending Title 5 issues related to funding and other issues that impacted the DSPS program statewide. I helped run meetings for counselors at the conference and helped present workshops to my college counterparts who had attended the conference. My CAPED affiliation added a great deal to my evolution as a DSPS counselor/coordinator as well as enhanced my ability to be creative and productive in advocating for students with disabilities. Years later, when I worked at Napa College, I would co-chair the annual convention and in 2009 received an award for my contributions to the organization. For over thirty years I have been extensively involved with CAPED and support its many causes.

In my new job I had to learn how to survive in an entirely different employment setting than I had experienced. The faculty groups I had contact with were very outspoken, and consensus on many issues was difficult to achieve. When I was in a room with dozens of faculty members, I rarely said anything because I believed my knowledge on most issues was not substantial enough to add to the debate. When I did speak, it was only about disability issues related to accommodations for my students. Another difference was that I had to work some weekends or late at night to attend board meetings, register students for new semester classes, or participate in special evening events. This was just an accepted part of the job.

It took me a while to learn how to function within this college structure. There are good people in every working group; however, there can also be those who thrive on the notion that their opinions and needs are more important than anyone else's and who will stop at nothing to get their own way even if it means destroying the lives of other employees. I look back at my five years at the college as helping me formulate and strengthen my resolve to maintain what I was and believed I could become, even if I faltered along the way.

In general, life was good. My family joined me in the fall of my first year at the college, when escrow closed on a house we had purchased. All of us thrived in the community and met wonderful people in the area and through the local Catholic church. We had an exceptional priest, and I remember vividly our many times together enjoying drinks and lively discussion. Like many Irish priests, he had immigrated to the U.S. to meet the demand for more Catholic clergy in this country. He was a people person and whether he was serious or happy, he loved and was always there for his parishioners. His memory lives on in my heart.

My family and I attended many dinners and other social events at the local church, and for the first time in my life, I felt a sense of community by attending masses and interacting with fellow churchgoers. When my son Michael was born in December of 1990, parishioners brought food and gifts to celebrate this new arrival. But soon after Michael was born, the social and employment foundations I was involved in ruptured.

As we turn various corners of our lives, we can find ourselves unprepared for the unexpected. If we believe in God, then we believe this supreme being has laid out before us the primary challenges of our lives. Even though things might go badly at the moment, we have an internal capacity along with our free will to overcome the adversity and go on. In his fine book, *The Road to Character,* David Brooks talks about how we can improve our character and encounter our own wisdom by looking at the big picture and moving away from our narcissistic attitudes and closed-mindedness. "Wisdom is not a body of information," he states. "It's the moral quality of knowing what you don't know and figuring out a way to handle your ignorance, uncertainty and limitations."

So, in 1989 and 1990, I quickly ascertained how the lack of wisdom had left me unprepared for the winds of change that would blow through my life. I was going along just fine, working hard to maintain a viable DSPS program. I met monthly with other community professionals to discuss the status of services available to disabled persons in the area. We exchanged information and developed strategies to improve the quality of lives for the people we represented. In addition, I created a recruitment program that allowed me to reach out well beyond our rural county and as far away as the San Francisco Bay Area, to encourage prospective students to consider attending the college. Another accomplishment was securing funds to enlarge and modernize the program's office space.

The DSPS program was housed in the lower level of one of the main classroom buildings, with two small offices that looked out over the surrounding meadows and hills. The main room was our computer lab, with desks and tables for special DSPS instruction. The number of students in the program grew each year. I asked the Industrial Arts instructor to draw up plans to increase the office space to include an accessible bathroom, one additional larger office for the DSPS coordinator, and a moderate size conference room. Then I approached the program manager in the chancellor's office to seek Title 5 funding. After months of discussion, I got the go-ahead. The college would put money into the project because they could justify using the conference room and bathroom for the general staff and student population. The woodshop instructor took on the job of constructing the additions. This was a major feather in my cap, and it made DSPS more integrated into the campus. This was completed in early 1989.

A few months later, in the summer of 1989, the college hired a new president/superintendent. A change of personnel at the top almost inevitably leads to personnel changes elsewhere in the institution, and hopefully for the best. As restructuring occurred, a new dean of student services was selected from the ranks of current staff and named to the position six months later. This person had neither the experience nor qualifications to lead a multi-disciplined student program.

Soon after that, the dean of the college called me into his office and told me he would begin the certification process to make me a tenured faculty member. He was frank in telling me he was going to be let go for no apparent reason and he wanted to take this action so I could retain my job. So, I became tenured and thought this might be the end of the story.

However, by the fall of 1990, further undercurrents of change got my attention. The dean was beginning to give the LD specialist more leverage in the program because she kept advocating for a better location with a quiet environment to test for potential learning-disabled students. Also, the dean wanted me to take more training to become a better DSPS coordinator. This was after I had become tenured, so the request made no sense. If I was not a good employee, why would they have tenured me?

The most obvious sign appeared in the spring of 1991, when I was away for a few days taking DSPS training at another community college campus. A counselor friend called with the news that a custodial crew had just moved my furniture out of my office and that the dean had given my office to the LD coordinator.

My new surroundings were in a closed off, windowless office that felt like a small storeroom. My supervisor tried to persuade me there was no other facility on campus to accommodate the LD specialist.

A few months later, I was placed in the fishbowl room right across from the office of the new Dean of Students. This made it difficult for me to run the program, because I was now on the upper floor with minimal contact with my staff. The LD specialist was gradually replacing me without benefit of a formal interview or intervention by the college president to stop this maneuver.

By law, the college was also supposed to provide me with a reader to help cover materials and submit reports as part of my job. Instead, I had to find a volunteer to help me do my assigned work. Then in August of 1991, the union rep informed me that the college administration wanted me to leave, and if I agreed I would receive a financial buyout of salary and benefits for one year. The fact that I was tenured prevented them from firing me outright.

I was shocked and despondent that I was no longer wanted at the college. I was performing at a high standard and doing as much as I could to advocate for and support students with disabilities. I was told by the rep that if I did not accept the administration's offer, I should expect to experience significant problems and potential dismissal in subsequent months. I attempted to discuss this matter with the president, but he was unwilling to speak with me.

The rep also told me not to discuss this matter with anyone but him. Of course, I discussed it with Eileen, Jay, and my other close friend at the time, John Crane. All were in accord that I should leave. They were afraid the pressure would become so severe my health might be jeopardized if I tried to fight back and challenge their actions. The fact is there was no way I could win this challenge and remain as an accepted and viable employee.

So, I made a counteroffer asking for at least two years of pay and benefits. In my field, employment opportunities were difficult to obtain and I knew it would take substantial time to find another job in the community college system. The administration agreed to a second year, but without benefits, and I agreed not to sue the college or make the agreement public. The college agreed to give an accurate and positive recommendation to any prospective employer who contacted them. I had substantial grounds to sue, given my disability. However, word would have gotten around and it would have been very difficult for me to be hired at another community college. I believe I made the best decision under the circumstances, because ultimately I was able to work at three more community colleges in the years that followed.

It was especially disturbing that both my immediate supervisor and the college president did not want to discuss this situation in person. So, on a September day in 1991, I gathered my belongings from my office and left the campus, heartbroken and still wondering what the hell was going on, since my job performance until then had never been questioned by my superiors.

Even though I later referred to this institution as the Peyton Place of the West, I met some very fine people at the college. A wonderful woman worked for me as a part time interpreter for the deaf, and during my last few months she served as my reader. I will never forget that during one of the last staff meetings I conducted, she sat next to me while the rest of the department members sat at the other end of the table. In their minds, I was no longer their program leader because word had gotten out that I would soon be leaving. Another wonderful colleague was the business and technology instructor, who encouraged me to move on with my life. And my brilliant staff assistant, who if she'd had a Master's degree in counseling, could have been the program director. She had stood by me as I struggled to grasp the many nuances of the program. Other people whose names I don't remember were very kind and supported my efforts at the college.

In conclusion, the problem was that a number of people who worked at the college became very protective of their turf. They would stop at nothing to make it difficult for others. Such behavior creates havoc and dysfunction in a public institution and overshadows what is good about that institution.

Chapter 10

Transition: In the Desert

Even though I was financially stable for a short period, my immediate and primary objective was to find another job as soon as possible. I had to restructure my resume, expand my network of professional contacts, and complete numerous long applications. Month after month, I sent applications to community colleges and Department of Rehabilitation offices throughout California. Because I lived in a rural area, I was continuously taking a bus or train to other parts of the state for interviews. When I was not selected for a position, I would feel depressed for days after the rejection, and on the verge of giving up. However, my natural optimism would return, propelling me to take up the mantle of courage and continue to apply for jobs. Even though I eventually found work, it would be another nine years before I would return to work full-time as a community college professional.

During this nine-year period, I was offered four positions, only one of which was at a community college. A year after I'd been let go, I accepted a temporary position at Victor Valley College (VVC) in the high desert of Southern California. This was a one-semester job as Coordinator/Counselor of the disabled students services program. In January of 1993, on the same date Bill Clinton was sworn in as forty-first president of the United States, I began working at the college. Eileen and her sister Terri had driven me to Victorville to find me a place to live. I did not know a soul in the area, but I soon made friends who were very helpful.

There were more pros than cons to accepting a one-semester position. First, I would be able to get off of Social Security and unemployment benefits. The job would allow me to maintain some credibility in coordinating a DSPS program, attend conferences, and expand a network of contacts that could render a big help down the road. As for cons, I would be away from home for a semester. I would miss my wife and children. It would cost more money to run two households, and traveling between Victorville and my family for visits took about two days by bus and train. As a family we discussed the cons, but there were no guarantees I would find a job closer to home. So, off I went.

On this job, I had the opportunity to write a Workability III Program grant through the Department of Rehab that would assist disabled students to develop job-seeking skills and find work during and after their tenure at a given college. The grant was approved. I immediately interviewed for the Workability III counseling position and worked an additional two years at the college, doing this job.

As a short-term employee at VVC, I experienced challenges and good times. I joke that I fulfilled my Catholic obligation of spending forty days and forty nights in the desert. The Dean of Students was of tremendous support as I tried to get the Workability program off the ground. However, politics came into play and the Dean was let go unexpectedly during my tenure.

In general, I enjoyed living in the Mohave Desert. There is a distinct beauty to the desert, with its diverse and seasonal plants and flowers. There is also a special quiet when you are walking in the wilderness. I usually slept well because the temperature dropped substantially from warm and hot during the day to a comfortable coolness in the late evening and early morning. Even though I missed my wife and family a great deal, I rate my experience in the California desert as a good one.

After two years on the project, the Department of Rehab decided to discontinue the grant because I was not placing enough students (called "consumers" in grant terminology) into gainful employment. I did place a few students, but a grant program of this type requires a number of years to get off the ground, and two years was not enough to attain the agreed upon goals.

There is always fallout from such decisions, especially for students who are adversely affected when specialized services are no longer available. Thus, again, I had to move on. All was not lost, however, because I was able to take these valuable work and personal experiences with me into other career opportunities.

In January 1996, I found myself living in Carson City, Nevada, working as administrator of a state agency, Services to the Blind and Visually Impaired. Two months prior to ending the job in Victorville, I had seen an announcement for this position. I knew the former director of the agency, who had encouraged me to apply for a counselor position when something opened up. He had just passed away when the position became available.

At the outset, I believed this opportunity might be a positive experience. I was a political appointee and served at the whim of a Bureau Chief (appointed by the governor of Nevada), responsible for administering numerous special state programs. My job was to coordinate and supervise the Services to the Blind and Visually Impaired program for the state of Nevada.

The political intrigue soon became apparent. It was a struggle from the beginning to learn the routine of running this specialized program and the personalities of the people I supervised. I reached out to staff, asked questions, promoted the program policies as best I could, and attempted to showcase my people skills in interactions with subordinates and clientele.

The assistant director of the program appeared to dislike me, told me he should have been chosen for my position, and did things behind my back to make me look bad. His advantage was that he could read the printed materials about program issues more quickly than I could. I needed a reader and was just learning how to become proficient with a computer. In fact, HR did pay an adaptive-computer specialist to help me learn the voice-assisted program. The assistant director protected himself by doing things to keep the program operational, yet at the same time made it look like I could never accomplish what he could. He did not have the best reputation, and a couple of years after I left he was fired for using program funds for his own benefit.

My secretary had excellent clerical skills but was caught up in office intrigue, and if it looked like my authority was in question, she would align with the person who was ultimately in charge. She was inadequate as my primary clerical support person.

Another person stole money from the petty cash fund and pleaded with me not to report her. The day my secretary alerted me to this, I asked to see the person immediately. She came into my office almost in tears. I forget why she said she stole the money. She was a single parent with two small children, and possibly was short of cash to pay a bill. I was very direct: Under no circumstances would I put up with theft. She was to put the money back immediately, and I would not take action at that time. She agreed, and I had no problem with her afterward.

As I made every effort to work through this social and political obstacle course, it became apparent this was probably not a workplace that would allow me to excel in the way I wanted. Even so, after being on the job for seven months, I was beginning to work through some of the adversity. I enjoyed visiting staff in other parts of the state and traveling with one of our rehab counselors to rural towns around the state to visit visually impaired clients and see firsthand the vital community resources serving the blind. I enjoyed my visits to the Las Vegas field office, where I trained staff and established a wonderful relationship with the program supervisor.

However, one Friday morning in late September of 1996, I was called into my supervisor's office and told that I was being let go. She provided no reason for my dismissal, and I was escorted out of the building with my belongings in hand. I should have known something negative was in the wind, because two weeks earlier the personnel director had called me in to HR to ask if I was sexually harassing one of my employees—the person who had been taking funds out of the till. This accusation was of course not true; I was fired due to innuendo and not because of an action I had committed. Hiring policy in Nevada offered me no protection to be reinstated, because I was a political appointee. After my dismissal, I had the opportunity to review my personnel file and found no negative remarks or reports to indicate why I had been fired. So, once again, and after only eight months on the job, I faced another transition period, and would look for an opportunity that would hopefully turn out much better than the Nevada experience. I still do not know the real reason I was fired from that job.

In the days that followed, my spirits were low, and I wondered what I would do next to support my family. My family had moved to Carson City in March of 1996, when we purchased a home there. Even though I received guidance from family and friends, during these periods of stress and dismay I still found myself alone walking through a tunnel of depression, questioning how things might have been different. When I stopped feeling sorry for myself, I began again to reestablish job contacts and intensified my efforts to reach out to people familiar with the job market I was interested in. It was crucial that I find a job sooner rather than later, given that my income resources were dwindling rapidly and I had five children to support, the youngest being six years old. Eileen was not working at the time, and it became apparent that any savings we had would be needed for this financial emergency.

My cousin Paul, also a graduate of the University of Santa Clara and a lawyer educated at the University of California, Berkeley, lived in Reno with his daughter Elizabeth. After several decades without seeing him, our paths crossed again when my family moved to Carson City. He often drove from Reno to Carson City to pick me up and take me to lunch. He is an integral part of our family, and his presence during that period was a gift. Over the years our relationship blossomed into a mutual respect and love, and countless times Paul has helped me with legal questions or other concerns. He is one of those special people who go out of their way to do good works without asking for anything in return.

Chapter 11

My Life Enriched with Private Sector Employment

A year later, in September of 1997, I finally found a job. I was hired by Hope Rehabilitation Services (HRS) in Monterey, California. Hope Services is a nonprofit organization whose mission is to serve the developmentally disabled through services ranging from independent living to placements in sheltered workshops and other employment programs. Sheltered workshops accommodate severely disabled people who cannot work in a competitive job. Usually, these workshops contract with commercial organizations to assemble products either by assembly line or piece by piece. Goodwill is an example of a company that operates sheltered workshops.

Headquartered in Santa Clara, California, Hope Services has served the community for decades, and at that time had received a Federal grant to provide janitorial workers at the U.S. Naval Postgraduate School in Monterey. I was hired as a job coach supervisor in this program, to monitor and provide support to make sure the janitorial contract was being fulfilled. Years earlier my buddy Jay had worked with Anna Foglia, Manager of Hope Services in Monterey. She had developed and secured the Navy contract. Jay recommended me, and Anna contacted me. I traveled to Monterey to interview for the position on a sunny fall day with fresh sea air in abundance and left Anna's office feeling highly optimistic. A few days later I was offered the job. I felt elated at the opportunity to work in a geographic area that I loved very much.

Even though I would not be making enough money to maintain two households, I took the job, thinking other doors might open for me as a result. Eileen decided to go back to work and began taking refresher courses to reinstate her nursing license for a job at the hospital in Carson City. I would miss my wife and children, but there was no way we could purchase a home in Monterey, given our financial strain. Again, I found myself as a part-time dad and husband.

At Hope, I was one of two or three people who supervised the job coaches, whose role was to help the most disabled workers learn and complete their assigned tasks. There were about six coaches, each with an assigned work area at the school. Job coach-assisted work groups (called enclaves) were assigned to clean the Naval buildings five days and nights a week. Most of the enclave workers were disabled and performed basic tasks that included sweeping floors, cleaning bathrooms, and emptying trash baskets. For more specialized jobs, such as waxing and stripping floors, and window washing that would be difficult for a person with a physical or mental impairment, Anna hired "client workers." Client workers were not usually disabled. All janitorial staff, about sixty in total, were Hope employees and received salaries and benefits.

Living and working in Monterey was a dream come true. The Monterey-Carmel area is one of the most beautiful places in the world, and I had always wanted to live near the ocean. The air is always fresh and most noticeable when a slight breeze blows in from the ocean. One of my favorite things was to walk along the bike trail from downtown Monterey, past Fishermen's Wharf, Cannery Row, the Monterey Bay Aquarium, and the Lovers' Point area adjacent to the bay.

On a clear day, I looked out into the blue ocean bay before me and imagined I could see forever. I couldn't see the waves, but I heard them moving against the shore, and the blue water appeared beautiful. I imagined the waves were tinged with blue and green and highlighted by the sun. On the fresh breeze I caught the fragrance of a nearby flower or tree, a reminder that they too should get some credit for the part they were playing in this spectacular experience. The natural beauty of the area almost guarantees revitalization of one's spirits.

Often, I would find a park bench and sit down to take in all that I was able to see and to reflect on my life in that tranquil environment. I would think not only about personal issues, but about the world. In that fall of 1997, I was probably in shock at the sudden death of John Denver, who died in a plane crash over Monterey Bay. One of his hobbies was flying small planes, and on his final flight he lost control of the aircraft due to engine problems and died when his plane hit the water. I considered Denver one of our greatest performers and songwriters. It had also been difficult for me and millions of others to deal with the untimely death of Princess Diana that August. Bill Clinton was beginning his second term as president and would soon have to deal with his Monica Lewinsky affair. Madeline Albright was sworn in as the first woman Secretary of State. On the business side of things, Woolworth's discount store would close its doors forever after being in business for over one hundred years. At the local movie theater, I might have considered seeing a popular movie of the time such as *Titanic, Anastasia,* or *As Good as It Gets.*

In this environment and against this cultural backdrop, I once again began learning new job skills, getting a grasp on new policies and procedures, and adjusting to a new employer's management style. I also had to adjust to working at night, which is when most of the janitorial work was completed. The night shift started at 3:30 pm and ended at 11:30 pm. By the time I arrived back at my apartment, it was after midnight. On my first day on the job, on the last Monday in September 1997, it was Indian summer, and I felt the hot afternoon sun on my back as I walked the two blocks to work. I had high expectations and wondered what this job had in store for me.

My tenure at Hope Services for almost three years allowed me to observe firsthand the wonderful things that can happen if you work for a program manager who is ethical and knows what she is doing. Anna Foglia is by far the best supervisor I ever worked for. She was a good listener, advocated for every one of her employees, and demanded quality performance from all of us. Anna went out of her way to make sure we had the resources and support to perform our assigned jobs. I was often asked to join her and other staff members for dinner, which would occur during my lunch hour on the night shift and at a location near the Navy School. Anna generously paid the total bill for countless meals many of us had with her over the years. I also enjoyed positive interactions with my coworkers.

In addition to the positive work environment, I developed a special awareness of how to work effectively with people who had developmental disabilities. All my prior experience had focused on educating and rehabilitating individuals whose disability required special accommodations and training. Properly assisting the developmentally disabled worker requires dedicated professionals determined to resolve employment issues with creativity and respect for their clients. Working at Hope Services enlightened me about how effective such a supported employment program can be, as I witnessed how many doors can be opened for this population through the persistent efforts of job coaches and the employers who ultimately hire them.

What I liked most about the job with Hope was that Anna allowed her employees to be creative and flexible in performing their jobs. Two job coach supervisors I worked with were Paul, the night shift lead supervisor and Dave, who worked day shift. Both were wonderful colleagues who I still see for lunch or dinner, usually in the company of Anna.

The Naval Postgraduate School campus is for Navy and other military personnel who are required to obtain advanced degrees in engineering, technology, business management, and liberal studies. The campus, which covers several acres and includes a small lake and path that circles the lake, is east of downtown Monterey, next to the Hyatt Resort Hotel. Today you must enter the campus through guarded gates, but when I worked there, you could walk through the gates without identification. The campus was designed around the administration building, which was an old hotel with a tremendously large ballroom. Most classroom buildings were more than two stories and the janitorial contract stipulated specific procedures for maintaining and cleaning the buildings. Part of my job was to learn where each building was located, what needed to be done and on what schedule, and alleviate any problems.

Hope's "client workers," who were mostly non-disabled, stripped and waxed floors and cleaned the more challenging areas. Since there were only a few job coaches and their work was with the folks with disabilities, many of these client workers were not always under direct supervision. As I began to observe key personnel every evening, and got to know individual workers, I was ultimately in a position to surprise some people who were sneaking off the premises and taking long lunch hours at a nearby liquor store or restaurant. One evening I went to the building of a client worker who was rumored to be doing just that. I waited until he returned from his lunch hour—much later than his work schedule mandated. He denied any wrongdoing. He was subsequently suspended for a day or two. The story here is not only about his questionable behavior, but also about his belief that because I was a visually impaired supervisor, he could get away with unacceptable behavior. His indiscretions were limited after that, but he would not speak to me unless I confronted him directly with a work issue. As with any job, we must always attempt to do the right thing and find creative approaches to enhance our effectiveness.

Most of the disabled people we worked with had mental difficulties. Some spoke in loud voices, and some had social impairments—for example, they might shake your hand longer than necessary or repeat a question to you without listening to your response. Most were friendly and worked hard to complete their assigned tasks. Some workers appeared highly introverted and kept to themselves, and it's possible they were autistic. Some individuals might have had some intellectual or developmental disability, along with autism. Once each month Anna held a client-staff meeting and invited all the workers. Those who came were delighted to be there to listen, talk with one another, and bring up any concerns they had. Given all their problems, people with intellectual disabilities especially came across in such a way that I wanted to do everything possible to help them move forward.

My custom during the evening shift was to make my rounds by walking through every building where janitorial work was being done. I had a special relationship with one client worker named Khang (pronounced Chang), who was assigned to a building off the beaten path. When I timed it right, I would run into him, sitting in the employee room, having a cup of hot tea. He would invite me to sit down and then pour me a cup of tea. Khang was an immigrant from Vietnam, attempting to support himself and his family in Monterey. He would sometimes talk about his childhood and family. He was kind, always cheerful, and optimistic. He was forthright and genuine and listened with his full attention. I often spent a good half-hour with him over tea, discussing family, politics, and his future. Khang was a model employee and, during my time in Monterey, he fell in love with a special lady. I was invited to their wedding reception, held in the ballroom of the Naval Postgraduate School—a venue Anna had pulled some strings to secure.

As I write about my interactions with Khang, I think about how different it is to work the evening shift compared to conventional daytime hours. At night, even though people are working, life seems to take a slower pace. The quiet of evening and darkness of night seem to influence our behavior. This is my subjective opinion, but having tea with Khang, and confronting the other client worker about his ethics on the job, and through other observations of clients with disabilities, it seems to me that behaviors are revealed more distinctly in the evening hours when we are tired, worn out, or just waiting for the eleventh hour to go home.

Khang was always calm, whether doing his work or sitting at a table drinking tea. The evening workers for the most part did not say much while they worked, and even on their breaks and lunch hour would rest and eat quietly. The end of the day means just that—we are slowing down. We struggle to stay alert and long for the moment when we will curl up in our beds for a restful sleep. Could there be a correlation between working well at a task and the darkness and calm of the evening adding something to our experience that makes the tasks more tolerable?

I not only enjoyed the work in Monterey, but enjoyed my time off the job as well. I would usually rise about 7:30 a.m. and go for a run on the bike trail or in my immediate neighborhood, or take a bicycle ride on the Monterey Bayside trail. I am not completely safe on a bicycle, but can ride slowly and only on a very smooth, wide, paved path that I know well. After the run (or ride) I would have until 3 p.m. to write letters, go shopping, or walk along the beach.

Whether it was sunny, windy, or foggy, I felt invigorated by the ocean air. I enjoyed walking from my apartment to do grocery shopping in downtown Monterey. The old-time drug store was still in operation, and the Safeway market was on the main thoroughfare for immediate access. Every Tuesday, I enjoyed walking to the local farmers market downtown to buy fresh vegetables, fruits, bread, and pastries.

I usually try to feel or hold the fruit or vegetable on my own, and then if I am unable to distinguish what I am after, I ask the vendor for help. Sometimes I cannot tell if an item is ripe or overripe. I have trouble seeing cobbed corn, good cauliflower, or green or purple cabbage. Most of the time at a farmer's market, I ask the vendor to pick out my items. I do have a good technique for finding a sweet watermelon: I tap the melon with my fist to determine the sound. A hollow sound tells me it's good. A dull sound, and I will leave it for the next customer to decide.

What was more gratifying than buying these fine organic foods, however, was getting to know the vendors. There were also special times when some of the Hope staff would meet Anna at the Hyatt Hotel sports bar. We would have a few drinks, hors d'oeuvres, and clam chowder, and talk shop or about our lives. Our job schedules often worked out so we could enjoy the highs and lows of Monday night football together.

No matter where I had lived for employment opportunities, I stayed in touch with my family in Carson City. We talked by phone at least once or twice a week. On long weekends, I traveled to see them and remained as long as I could. When I worked for a public institution such as a community college, school holidays and vacations usually occurred at the same time, allowing more time for mutual visits—family coming to Monterey or me venturing to Nevada. My children were growing up: Monica was 24, Carolyn was 22, Jenny was 20, Laura was in high school, and Michael was 12 years old playing in little league and loving video games. One or more of my daughters would drive to Monterey, stay a few days, then drive me back with them to Carson City. Those were fun times. Eileen would sometimes visit with a girlfriend and attend a local retreat or just relax. Rarely did everybody come at once. I also had other friends who traveled to visit me during that time.

Despite the rewards of the job, there were days when I felt the pressure of supporting two households. Money was scarce, and Eileen had gone back to a job after ten years of not working. Nonprofit salaries cannot compare with the pay scale at state or community colleges, and I began to think about finding another job. As I walked through the buildings at the Navy School, and occasionally observed a class in session, I knew I would not be content unless I returned to working for a community college. My heart was not in being a job coach supervisor or program manager for the rest of my work life. I wanted to be a student advocate and counselor again. Working in academia was my true calling.

I hated to think this way, because I loved the work and cherished my time under the tutelage of Anna's management style and friendship. In the meantime, Anna had asked if I would write a Department of Rehab grant to address supported employment issues for mentally impaired clients. Of course I agreed. The grant was approved, and I was hired as grant manager in mid-July of 1998. Happily, I returned to working days instead of evenings. I also had responsibility for supervising a job coach who was invaluable in supporting me as we attempted to place clients into gainful employment.

The new job was an extension of Hope services and was in nearby Pacific Grove, within walking distance of Monterey. Anna relocated there as well. I enjoyed the work, and my office had a big window that allowed in a lot of sunlight, which felt much better than working in an enclosed office with florescent lighting.

My mandate was to establish a job placement program to assist client referrals from the Department of Rehabilitation for training and job placement. This would mean working in conjunction with the DOR counseling staff in the area to focus upon the particular job or training goal agreed upon by the designated consumer (worker) and their counselor. This plan is referred to as the IWRP, which stands for Individual Work-related Rehabilitation Plan. My primary responsibility was to work directly with clients to evaluate their knowledge, skills, and abilities, and apply their job goals and motivation levels to an employment opportunity for which they qualified. As a former rehabilitation counselor, I felt right at home with job development activities, which entailed going into the community and contacting employers to offer them qualified candidates for their job openings.

The primary task of the job developer was to convince prospective employers that people with disabilities can perform effectively and productively on the job. The key to success is to make sure the client/consumer possesses the necessary skills to perform the job.

Usually, when the Department of Rehab refers a client to a vendor like Hope Services, a rehab plan has already been written. Even so, I would sit down with the client/consumer and discuss and set specific goals and objectives to prepare this person to obtain and keep a job. With every client, the plan is different. Preparation might include learning how to write a resume, contact employers, dress for the job, and most importantly—interview effectively. Neila, my job coach, would work with the clients on some of these tasks. On this grant, I sometimes had 25 students at a time on my caseload. I was only able to find jobs for maybe 20 percent of them. During each visit with my clients, I would write a report that went into their files. If a problem occurred, I would contact their rehab counselor to discuss the matter, which would generate a meeting of the counselor, client, and me.

I loved the challenge of walking into an employer's office to discuss their hiring needs and ask if they would consider offering a job to a person with a disability. Many times I hit a brick wall—under no circumstances would they hire a person with what they called a "handicap." However, when an employer was interested, the world became a better place, and I was excited to pass the good news to my clients, with the stipulation they would have to interview for the position and then demonstrate on the job that they could perform and live up to the employer's expectations.

The second factor to guarantee successful job placement was to identify any accommodations the worker would need in order to perform the job. The DOR could purchase such accommodations, from special aids and equipment such as tape recorders and closed circuit TVs with print magnification, to paying for transportation costs such as gasoline or issuing bus passes. Accommodations address the functional limitations based on the person's disability. Readers, interpreters, and drivers are other types of assistance. At the Navy school, job coaches were available to teach and instruct mentally impaired workers to perform the job tasks they were assigned. Without this accommodation, there would have been no contract at the Navy school for disabled folks. Employers could also receive federal tax credits, and the DOR could provide on-the-job training or funds to help pay the client's salary for the first two to three months. Most employers had no idea about these crucial incentives.

In addition, our program offered job coaching support for the client/worker as long as the person needed it. Neila was highly skilled at supporting workers as they learned their tasks. Plus, she was a tremendous support to me and always backed me up when it came to working with employers. Sometimes she would drive me to a specific location, especially in rural areas. She would also read through client files for me and sit in on many of my client meetings to serve as a notetaker or just be present so the client would get to know her and understand what she did as a job coach. I respect Neila's professionalism and expertise as she continues assisting Hope Rehab clients in the Monterey area to attain a better quality of life and make a living.

I could share countless success stories about placing clients into gainful employment, but two people remain particularly in my mind.

One was a Hispanic client in the Soledad region who I'll call Miguel. His parents, who I visited in their home, were very supportive of their son, but not optimistic about his ability to hold a job, given his mental disability. Neila and I traveled all over the area trying to place our star client. There are lessons to be learned from every job development effort, and in this case, I knocked on numerous employer doors. I contacted public agencies like EDD and the HR department at Soledad State Prison.

What I did not realize was that people in the community had no idea whether or not they could trust me. I was a stranger in their rural town, trying to persuade employers to take a chance on hiring a young man with a disability. Eventually I met with the food service operator at the Soledad Correctional Training Facility, where they needed a young person to bus tables and perform related food service tasks. The supervisor agreed to take a chance on Miguel, and he was eventually hired with minimal support from Neila.

It was so rewarding to observe him working at his job and being productive. His parents were very proud and Miguel and other clients were honored for their employment success at a special public luncheon sponsored by DOR. After the event, Miguel and his parents presented me with a nice money clip that I still have. Another factor for the successful outcome of placing workers like Miguel has to do with maintaining your professionalism even when the situation appears bleak—you need to keep pursuing your efforts and not give up on what you started. I am pleased that I helped make a difference for Miguel, though he did most of the work.

In addition to this work at Hope Services, I volunteered to conduct monthly meetings for the Monterey County Committee for the Employment of People with Disabilities (MCCEPD). The committee was a satellite organization of the State Governor's committee by the same name. Our mission was to invite employers and other community professionals to discuss how to improve their hiring of qualified workers with disabilities. I met a diverse segment of community members and served as the committee chair for one year.

One of our projects was to invite local mayors to a luncheon meeting at a downtown hotel. When the master of ceremonies did not show up, I had to take over and run the show. I was so nervous. My friend Paul from the Navy School brought me a Manhattan from the bar to calm my nerves. I had Toastmaster experience, but in this case I had to conduct the event by the seat of my pants. I will never forget that after the meeting, my friend Deborah from the Department of Rehab congratulated me and encouraged me to move my career beyond the Hope Services program. Deborah knew my frustrations at not being in a community college, and her encouragement kept me moving in that direction.

Serving as MCCEPD chair for one year enhanced my leadership abilities and afforded me experience that propelled me into more challenging roles in subsequent years. I even met California congressman Sam Farr, who was a strong advocate for hiring people with disabilities. At our meetings he encouraged employers to hire qualified disabled people who, if given an opportunity, could prove an employer had made the right decision. These committee forums opened doors to employment opportunities. The disappointing reality is that the employment rate of people with disabilities in the United States is still marginal compared to what it should be. The challenge still remains to identify alternative and creative ways to open employment doors for this segment of the population.

The second story demonstrates what can occur when you least expect it. On one occasion, I walked into a large chain grocery store in Monterey and met with the store manager. I explained the purpose of my visit and inquired if there were any job openings for courtesy clerks—workers who help bag groceries. She stated there were no openings and began to lecture me on how she had no time to train an individual with a disability. The conversation ended abruptly, and I left the store upset and thinking about how to approach this manager again when she was having a better day.

At the time, I was trying to place a young woman in an entry level position at a pet store chain, as a pet assistant, which involved caring for and grooming cats and dogs. I had guided her through a screening test that, by its design, was a waste of time. Many people with mental disabilities have difficulty understanding written questions without an interpretation. Rather than write their answers, a client should have an opportunity to interview orally with a store manager. My client was not selected for the position.

A few weeks later, I heard she had been hired as a grocery store courtesy clerk—at the same store where I had run into the agitated supervisor. I scheduled an appointment to visit my client and the store manager who hired her. I was surprised to find out that not only was my client doing a fine job, but the supervisor had nothing but good things to say about her. In fact, my client had found the job on her own and did not require job coaching. The lesson here is to never make assumptions about an employer's behavior until a job placement is finalized.

As the twentieth century was coming to a close, I knew more strongly than ever that a change was in the works. I would have to move on with my career and return to work as a Coordinator of a Disabled Student Services program at a community college. I wanted so much to remain on the Monterey Peninsula and continue working for Anna, but I knew in my heart that my life's work was to support students with disabilities. Thus, I began applying for positions that became available in the region.

In the meantime, I supplemented my income by providing specialized training to professionals in the area who worked with people with special needs. I spent one entire Saturday presenting disability awareness training to special education employees in the Salinas school district. The workshop earned me a much-needed hundred dollars for a few hours of work on the weekend. I used the Windmills training, in which I had become certified at Victor Valley College. This training helps employers understand that people with disabilities can perform as well as or better than nondisabled employees. Experiential activities in this training gave participants the opportunity to examine their fears and biases about interacting with or hiring people with mental, physical, or sensory impairment. Exchanges in the classroom break down attitudinal barriers in front of people's eyes. Participants emerge from the training as new believers in why they should, rather than should not, hire qualified people with disabilities.

Then, as the new century arrived, I finally was invited to an interview with Evergreen Valley College in San Jose, California. I was eventually chosen for the DSPS Coordinator position and in July of 2000 began another chapter of my life journey. Anna and my counterparts at Hope gave me a wonderful going away party, and many people in the community attended the event. It was a special moment in my life.

It was just before I left Monterey that I completed my first marathon, as I along with my good friend and former roommate

Ron (from Monterey) completed the 26.2 mile Big Sur marathon. I crossed the finish line wearing my Hope Rehabilitation T-shirt and with a smile on my face. Anna was there to congratulate me and offer water and other amenities. So, I left behind Monterey, but not the friendships and memories.

Chapter 12

Another Transition

As I moved on to another career challenge, I felt excitement, yet my heart was heavy with regret that I was no longer in Monterey working with the people I had come to respect and care for so much. I had moved temporarily into my parents' house in San Mateo, which was closer to San Jose than Monterey, but unless I commuted with someone who worked at Evergreen Valley College, it took me over two hours to get to and from work on public transportation.

It had also been over five years since I had worked in the community college system. I quickly ascertained that I had plenty of catching up to do to understand this particular DSPS program. I also had to learn the nuances of the internal workings of the college.

Basically, a DSPS Coordinator monitors the program budget, advocates for and implements accessibility standards for students and college employees with disabilities, and coordinates advisory committee meetings with representatives from community agencies to address issues related to the program mission. It became clear from the outset that as a program coordinator, I had been given minimal authority to make major decisions relevant to this specially funded program. The dean of students was smothered with responsibilities as a program administrator, and her leadership was largely absent. I could advocate for budget changes, but I had no authority to override budget decisions.

My staff included a program secretary, a learning disability specialist, an academic advisor, and a speech pathologist. All were skilled and supported the students they served. However, some of them tried to undermine my efforts and often would not support my approach to get things done. Weekly staff meetings were always a challenge, but I did hold it together and came through with marginal success. At the outset, I had to refresh myself regarding Title V regulations, and I had to obtain help to learn the adaptive technology in order for me to access the computer.

The college paid for a specialist to train me to use JAWS, which is software that enables the blind and visually impaired to respond to a voice screen-reader. The training is intense, but because there are so many commands required to become proficient on the computer, I fell short. I could respond to email and write letters and some documents, but did not excel at reading charts or perusing the internet as sighted people are able to do. Even if I had been more proficient with the computer and adaptive technology, I would have needed a secretary or a reader with computer skills to proofread my work and make corrections under my direction.

Then there was the issue of the college providing me with a support person to address some of the clerical and other issues that require sight to perform. Evergreen Valley College was one of two campuses that made up the Evergreen district. The other was San Jose City College. The coordinator of the San Jose City College DSPS program had a hearing impairment and was supported with accommodations (clerical support and interpreters) because of the impairment. For whatever reasons, the EVC district office business officer would not allocate funds for accommodating me, and my boss and the college president did not believe my disability issues were a priority. I had to rely on what was available to me. It was disappointing and discouraging.

Had it not been for the director of HR in the district office, who could see I was in a no-win situation, I don't know what I would have done. She came to my office once or twice a week for about an hour-and-a-half and helped with reading my mail and completing some of my pending paperwork. Without her, I can only speculate what might have happened to me.

The point here is that Title V funding cannot be used for reasonable accommodation support of employees who are eligible. However, by ADA mandates, employers who hire qualified people with disabilities must provide reasonable accommodations when necessary to perform essential job tasks. It is the responsibility of every community college district to set aside funding to address these accommodations. Although I could use a computer with some adaptive software, I still needed clerical support to complete important job tasks. Despite these struggles, I tried to focus on the concept that there would be light at the end of the tunnel.

To monitor the program budget, I was continuously sitting with the college business officer to discuss how to resolve major monetary issues. Since the Evergreen campus did not serve as many students, most of the state allocation went to the City College DSPS program. This was fair to some extent, but the district business officer at times approved moving line item funds that had been designated for the Evergreen campus, to what he deemed more pressing issues at City College. I was not informed of these changes, which made it difficult to manage my own budget. It is astonishing to me now that I endured almost four years at the helm of this program. In fact, I received tenure during that period by working extra hard and because of my personal mandate to perform at or above a satisfactory level.

There are always political issues when you work for a college or state program. Somehow you have to rise above the chaos and do the best you can.

As with all the jobs I held, I met special individuals who helped and supported me through bad and good times. My friend Myron often helped me convert forms and work documents into Braille, made sure the JAWS software was operating properly, and helped me access email and other computer applications. The business program dean and the wonderful VP of student services offered consultation and encouragement that propelled me to keep moving forward. Marianne, the speech pathologist, taught me a great deal about what a program coordinator must do to be an effective leader. Her candid and valuable input meant a lot to me in those dark days. Liz, the program secretary, went out of her way to assist me with job priorities when other people were not available. When I began to apply for other jobs, Harvey from the counseling department sometimes came to my home and helped me complete tedious job applications for other community college positions.

I did enjoy some success as I gradually expanded the proactive Disabled Advisory Committee. I recruited rehab professionals and college staff to meet quarterly to discuss improvements to the DSPS program. At one full-day event I had the honor of introducing the Director of the statewide DOR, Catherine Canpisi, at the opening session. During that day, I interacted with local DOR administrators and counselors I had worked with when I began my career in 1972. Such advisory committees can be a viable resource to a DSPS program and can nurture, support, and appreciate people who support community inclusion.

A year and a half into the Evergreen job, I had moved back to Monterey, into a studio apartment across the street from the Monterey Bay. Even though the commute to San Jose was longer, it was much easier carpooling with friends than struggling with train, bus, and light rail to get to work. In Monterey, I lived for the weekends, when I could unwind by taking ocean walks and listening to music. Fresh sea air is always invigorating, and weekends brought me profound stress-free moments. From time to time, I visited with Anna and other friends as well as family. It was always special when my son Michael came to visit. We did many things together but especially had fun just throwing the football around and talking.

Harvey, who lived nearby, often drove an extra twenty minutes to pick me up at my apartment complex and take me all the way to San Jose. I met my special friend Phil, from Pacific Grove, on the shuttle bus from Gilroy to Monterey. Phil worked in Sunnyvale for a semiconductor manufacturer. His four children were in college or starting their own families, and I quickly became part of his extended family. We were both Democrats and loved talking politics and history, listening to classical music, and eating at fine restaurants, his favorite being French cuisine at Fifi's in Pacific Grove. We also hiked along the coast near Asilomar. Phil often went out of his way to give me a ride or share some CDs with me. He was a beacon of light in my life, and I will always cherish his friendship and the good times with him and his family. He often gave me a ride to my apartment from Gilroy to Monterey when the shuttle service was not in operation. Phil passed away unexpectedly in October 2016. I miss him very much.

Despite the stresses of the job, ultimately I began to feel more comfortable handling day to day operations of the program. I enjoyed numerous and productive interactions with students and with the college administration. I expanded my horizons by actively participating in CAPED conferences and building bridges with my counterparts from DSPS programs at other colleges. I made two presentations to the College Board of Trustees to articulate the status and productivity level of Evergreen Valley's DSPS program.

I always had difficulty managing the budget and submitting the annual program reports to the state chancellor's office, and had to rely on others to gather data and other information to complete the task. At times I just could not clearly comprehend the many issues that pervaded the landscape. I had to overcome peer criticism, unfair challenges, and at times ridicule from those who felt they could have done a better job. At times, I might be slow on the uptake, but give me time to grasp a concept or an issue, and I can fight in the ring with any adversary. My disability has always been that I have been unable to acquire and process information in an abbreviated period of time. I have to rely on the printed word and at times need to depend on a sighted person to convey the printed word to me and to check my writing in terms of presentation and conceptual formatting. I did the best I could, sought the counsel of others when it seemed necessary, and survived the onslaught of negativity by rising above it all. I was listening to Frank Sinatra sing "I Did It My Way" during that period. As I see it, I took the blows, survived the lows, fought the adversity, and triumphed by doing it my way.

The added security of attaining tenure in early 2004 at Evergreen was a feather in my cap, but at the same time, I knew I must move on. A few months earlier, in November 2003, I had applied for a Workability III counselor position at Napa Valley College. In mid-February I interviewed for the position and was offered the job. I had about five weeks to terminate my job at Evergreen Valley College, settle things in Monterey, and find a place to live in Napa.

With the help of my buddy Jay, we found an apartment in Napa near a bus stop and a shopping area. There was even a bike and walking trail next door to the complex, which showcased a tributary of the Napa River. In mid-March, my daughter Carolyn, who had given birth to my second grandson, Keegan Michael, a month before Christmas, arrived with her newborn to clean my Monterey apartment and help me move to Napa. (My first grandson, Donovan, had been born in July 1999, to Monica.) Those two days during which father, daughter, and grandson spent quality time together made my last moments in Monterey special. From there, it was on to Napa Valley College, where my career would close on a positive note and eventually a transition into retirement with high spirits and the satisfaction that I had given my best in multiple diverse work environments and made a difference in the lives of both employers and students.

Chapter 13

Days of Wine and Roses in Napa

Napa, in the heart of Northern California's wine country, was not new to me. When I was ten years old in August of 1954, I attended Enchanted Hills, a summer camp for blind children and adolescents. The experience changed my life. I slept in a sleeping bag and open cabins under the stars, where I could even see a few dots of light through the high trees. The camp was surrounded by tall redwood trees, beautiful specimens of nature even though I could not fully see them. The air was fresh, the food delicious, and every night we met in the redwood glen for storytelling and singing around the campfire. During the day we swam, rowed boats, rode horses, and made crafts with clay and leather. The most memorable experiences involved meeting others my age and interacting with campground staff. All of us blind campers felt accepted and welcomed by the staff. At first I felt fearful and inadequate talking with peers and sighted staff members, but as the days passed I developed confidence. The experience made me more open to enjoying relationships with sighted people. I attended Enchanted Hill for seven summers.

In retirement, I would return to this unique place in the Napa Hills as part of the camping staff, to engage a new generation of blind campers and witness their excitement and joy. There is something magical about Enchanted Hills, as you wake up under the redwoods to the call of blue jays and other birds. The camp was devastated by the Napa Fire in 2017, and rebuilding will continue for several years. Part of who I am originates from the special camp experiences in those formative years of my life. My childhood Napa experience was a good omen, and I looked forward to living and working in the Napa Valley environment.

I began my new job with anticipation and high expectations. I did not report directly to the Workability program supervisor, but to faculty personnel who comprised my tenure evaluation committee. The Workability III program administrator had developed an excellent program to support the academic and job placement needs of student referrals from the Department of Rehabilitation. In addition to being the Workability III job developer, I had direct responsibility for developing education plans for college students who were being supported by the DOR. The major part of my job was to identify classes these students needed for graduation or transfer to a four-year college. The program employed a full-time secretary, a program tutor/basic skills instructor, and student aides.

The spirit of cooperation and acceptance of diversity was a pervasive reality on campus, and I immediately felt very much a part of the college. Of course, there were personality conflicts, territorial issues, and people who made it difficult for everyone else. But in general, my tenure at NVC was a very positive experience. I felt secure and accepted as a colleague who had something to offer.

The year 2004 was eventful in many ways, both personal and social. The summer Olympics was held in Athens, and in October the Boston Red Sox swept the St. Louis Cardinals to win the World Series. Cinemagoers were entertained by the popular Million Dollar Baby and Phantom of the Opera. That year saw the passing of former president Ronald Reagan, as well as Marlon Brando and Rodney Dangerfield. Newspaper headlines noted the U.S. presidential election, the Iraq war, and the terrorist bombing in the Madrid subways on March 11.

Also during 2004, in late August, my father, Sam Dana, passed away at eighty-four. My father was a good man even though he had a bad temper. His generation thrived on hard work and doing whatever was necessary to help family and friends. He had grown up in San Francisco to parents who were born in Italy. He lived his life to the fullest even though he had a difficult upbringing with a very strict father. He became a professional systems analyst, and in his spare time repaired cars, renovated houses, laid bricks, welded, and loved to play basketball even though he stood only five-foot-nine. He was also a small-game hunter and avid fisherman. He could do anything he put his mind to.

My father and I were not especially close, but I did love him. And after I accepted that we would never have that special father/son relationship, I was able to maintain a rapport with him. This metamorphosis came about as I learning to be a father myself. I was never going to change my dad, but I learned to accept his good qualities and cherish the special moments between us—moments when I was a child and he would ask me to rub his back at night, or when I was an adolescent and he would invite me to sit down and talk to him while he was laying bricks in the backyard. He had his faults, but he was social and friendly, had many funny stories to tell, and did the best he could to live a good life.

I will never forget his first visit to the home Eileen and I had purchased in Hayward. The garage had been converted into a family room and renovated kitchen, and he gave me hell for buying a home that didn't have a garage. The irony is that he had never used his own garage to store a car. His double-car garage was and still is full of not only his tools but other junk that should have been thrown away years ago. I think of my father often and wonder what might have been if the barriers between us had not been so impactful. I told myself that if I ever had a son, I would make every effort to love him and be open to his needs and wants and would let him know my love for him was unconditional. My son Michael and I have just this kind of relationship.

By the time of Dad's death, I had spent almost six months on the NVC campus. The college was in a growth mode, adding a science building, a library, and a performing arts center. When family and friends came to visit, we would visit the local wineries, go biking in the nearby hills, enjoy local restaurants, and tour beautiful parts of San Francisco.

The high point of my job was to witness my students' progress as they attended classes and trained for jobs. I welcomed the challenge of developing myself into an effective and productive academic counselor. I thrived on the consultations with my peers to address and resolve tricky academic issues in support of students. Aside from the countless meetings and training sessions on my schedule, I always took time to work out in the weight room or enjoy a two- or three-mile run in the parks and fields around the campus. There was always a strong breeze and I enjoyed hearing the birds sing and a distant train pass as I challenged myself in a physical workout. I almost titled this manuscript "Running for Your Life" because I believe running almost daily has helped keep me fit and healthy. My office had a good-sized window and I always felt refreshed when I could take a few moments to just look out at the nearby trees and bushes.

It was also rewarding to build viable relationships with college faculty and staff. I became friends with Stephanie Burns, for example, the new biology instructor with an office next to mine. She supported the accommodations students needed and we worked together to resolve our mutual students' academic issues. I applaud her for her compassion and directness in supporting students whether they have disabilities or not. Dean Ehlen, the Machine Shop instructor, went all out to support my students in his classes. He provided me with employer contacts in the community and made sure his students with a disability were extended reasonable accommodations. Both he and Stephanie expected students with special needs to make the effort to complete assignments and take the necessary preparation to pass exams. There were no exceptions to this policy. He kept me apprised of the progress of every one of my students in his classroom. The more often teaching faculty come in contact with student diversity issues and students with sensory, physical, or mental impairment, the stronger the likelihood of successful outcomes for both instructors and students.

Any credit I take for helping my students succeed at the college must be shared with John Adams, a Department of Rehabilitation counselor housed in the Napa office. John often came to my office to discuss his Workability III clients who were attending NVC. If a student was missing classes or not taking advantage of the accommodations offered, we would meet with the student in my office to gain the student's perspective and offer constructive resolutions. Often, the student left those meetings with a different perspective and the ability to move forward. Our goal was ultimately to place our mutual consumers (clients) and students into gainful employment. As a young boy, John had lost one of his legs in a train accident. His perspective and determination made him into one of the most productive and sincere professionals I have ever met. We learned from each other and developed a close friendship.

In nearly twenty years of service in the community college system, I was fortunate to meet highly skilled colleagues and professionals who were willing to share their experience and knowledge with me. It made no difference to them that I was not a generalist counselor (someone who works with students who do not require special assistance) because the bottom line was that as a peer, I too was attempting to make a positive difference for students. It is one thing to attend staff meetings and college-wide training workshops; it is another to take time to really engage with our peers on different levels. I was fortunate to get to know people who accepted me and invited me to participate in activities beyond our work environment. Reciprocal friendship is gold.

Rebecca Scott, Gwen Kell, and Oscar De Haro are others with whom I had the good fortune to share special moments away from NVC and the routine of work. These folks demonstrated to me that they cared about who I was and that my disability made no difference to them.

Rebecca coordinates the college library and has jurisdiction over the disabled student services program. We hit it off right away. Her candid and positive approach to everything makes her special. She is an excellent workshop facilitator and we still meet for lunch from time to time to catch up on our lives.

Gwen Kell is a compassionate and brilliant counselor who for many years has worked in the college transfer center. We took many lunchtime walks together, talking about college issues, family matters, and life. Once she invited me to take a kayak ride on the Napa River. The day was warm and clear and the excursion required a two-person effort to navigate the kayak along parts of the river. Gwen rowed from the back as our navigator, and I helped row as needed from the front. I remember so well how the water flowed up against the boat. The splashes from the movement of the oars was a natural sound that made me want to keep moving forward on the waterway. I heard the distant sound of vehicles on the Napa streets and the distant birds singing their familiar tunes. It was remarkable to find myself gliding on the river in a kayak, seeing the world from a different perspective.

Gwen will always be a beacon of light in my life for the examples she sets and the unconditional kindness she has always shown me.

As a faculty member, I always tried to maintain positive relationships with college administrators who at times had to make difficult decisions that did not please everyone. I was able to befriend Oscar De Haro, who was and at the time of this writing is vice-president of student services. It was my good fortune to get to know Oscar as a friend. We enjoyed talking sports and sharing ideas on how we could influence change on campus. Oscar had my back when one of my students filed a complaint about me and called for my termination. The student had a mental problem and had misunderstood a comment I made about a medication she was taking. I had to attend a meeting with Oscar and the student and hear out her issues. Afterward, Oscar told me not to worry, my job was not in jeopardy, and the student had invalid assumptions about her allegations. Oscar was always there to advise and support me. In my opinion, he is a primary example of an enlightened person who will apply both objective and compassionate approaches as he performs his many job responsibilities.

Always, my most gratifying moments have been to witness the progress of students. I can tell many stories of students who rolled into my office in a wheelchair or arrived with a white cane or guide dog, seeking help with an academic or personal issue. I learned quickly how essential it is to objectively assess student problems and implement a viable game plan to support their specific goals. I always provided my students with the utmost attention and courtesy as I attempted to develop an education plan they could follow toward a degree. If we are to win over disabled students to the value of post-secondary education, we must recognize their perception of how they will fit into the academic and social community. We must go with the flow when it comes to assisting our students. We must challenge them to challenge themselves to take advantage of the special accommodations to ensure their access to materials, resources, and special equipment intended to guarantee them an equal playing field.

As I reflect upon students I have assisted through the years, I forget their names but remember their faces and why they came to me for support. A few stories (using fictional names) typify what has made my career challenging and interesting.

The first is about Bryan, a paraplegic who got around using a wheelchair. He wanted to attend the University of California at Berkeley and had enrolled at NVC to obtain an Associate degree in science. He was a brilliant student and earned a B average at Napa. Bryan convinced me right away that he would be a success no matter what he strived to do. He was a Rehab client and took advantage of every opportunity presented him. He was eventually accepted at Berkeley, and I have no doubt he is employed or in graduate school somewhere. His goal was to become a federal employee in the sciences, preferably meteorology or space.

I mention Bryan not only because of his academic accomplishments, but also because he challenged me to research and arrange for him to meet the contacts and recruiters who would facilitate his transition to the university. He had the ability to do such research on his own, but it was my job to find out what was required to help him make a successful transition. I had no experience helping students get into UC Berkeley and had to discuss the matter with colleagues who knew the process. At times, it seemed like I was a student once again, having to research special academic transfer requirements to move forward. Bryan will never know how much he taught me about going the extra mile to ensure he would make the transition to a university venue.

Then there was Sarah, who had a learning disability. She was a business major and wanted to become a clerical support person in an office. She was a Department of Rehab referral and required academic counseling as well as job development and placement services. I contacted local employers and finally arranged a job interview for her with the local Red Cross office. Sarah didn't show up for the interview. She later informed me that her religious beliefs did not allow her to work for an organization that dealt with blood donations. I was upset with her, not because of her beliefs, but because she had failed to tell me before I set up the interview. To my knowledge, Sarah never did consider other job options. I learned never to assume that a job opportunity was assured until a student was offered the position and showed up to begin work.

In my view, student success depends upon a multiplicity of factors and how effectively each student handles specific situations. I think of this as a student mystique that requires accepting students as individuals, each with their own set of attributes and concerns about what they want to do and where they want to go. The college professional (the counselor) has to nurture the student's development by objectively listening to their issues, respecting confidentiality, and providing accurate information about course requirements, medical reports, or other assessments. The counselor must keep an open mind and strive to win the student's trust to help them recognize what they must do to succeed.

I was always impressed how many of my nursing students, most of whom, in addition to their physical disability, had learning disabilities due to dyslexia, or dyscalculia, which could affect their ability to study math, chemistry, and biology. Some also had psychological disabilities such as depression or bipolar disorder.

These students laid everything on the line, even when the odds were often against them, to be accepted into the nursing program. Not only did they have to pass English, anatomy, and other science courses, they also had to overcome obstacles and challenges brought about by their physical impairments. I was fortunate to have many successes in my students being accepted into the nursing program. The challenges these students faced at the beginning of the training process no doubt provided excellent learning opportunities as they continued through nursing programs and applied for jobs. Whatever academic or vocational program our students aim for, they have to learn how to adjust to adversity, overcome despair, and strive to meet commitments. They become aware how much their attitudes and outlook factor into putting their best selves forward in living with their disabilities as they come to the threshold of attaining their goals.

At times, we must use tough love with our students, and when that works and these students hold their heads high at the commencement ceremony, the college professionals directly involved with them can also smile and take pride in witnessing their ultimate memorable moment, as well as take some pride in a job well done.

Besides being a passionate student advocate, I always made it a priority to help bring about disability awareness issues on campus. I strongly believe those who have disabilities must make every conscious effort to educate others about disability issues, rights, and laws that mandate access into the mainstream of society. At NVC I helped form a Disabled Advisory Committee of faculty, classified staff, and students whose mission was to create channels of acceptance and awareness that would create a more barrier-free campus. I invited community professionals to attend meetings and offer their input. To my surprise, the president/superintendent of NVC always took time in his busy schedule to attend these meetings. Chris McCarthy understood diversity issues and wanted to correct misconceptions and ensure that every student, disabled or not, received equal opportunity to succeed academically. As I recall, Chris had lost a substantial part of his vision earlier in his life. He told me this experience taught him to accept that he would need to make certain adjustments to his daily life. Chris lent credence and vitality to the advisory committee.

Every year in October, which is National Disabilities Awareness month, we held special events and workshops for students, staff, and the community. When he could, Chris offered remarks during the opening proceedings. The master of ceremonies role always seemed to fall in my lap, I guess because I was the committee chair. I was also a bundle of nerves when I had to introduce people and mediate panel discussions. In my view, these community forums were always successful. Any time you bring people together from diverse backgrounds to share their perspectives on how they live with an impairment can only result in positive outcomes. My coworkers worked diligently behind the scenes to arrange for food and refreshments and make sure meeting locations were properly set up and accessible. I was relieved when these affairs were over and I could take pride in their success based on feedback from attendees.

So, as the year 2010 unfolded, after six years at NVC, I began to sense that something different and good was going to happen to me. It was similar to being at or listening to a baseball game where the Giants are up for their last at bat at the bottom of the ninth inning. They are trailing by one run, with two runners on base with two outs. The excitement in the ballpark is mounting as the last batter takes his swings.

In a similar way, I was in this position when it came to Wednesday, May 26, 2010, my last day of work at a community college. I was at the end of my work responsibilities. The ninth inning for me was over. The question was, did I strike out, or did I hit a home run to win the game? As I see it, I did not hit the home run, but I did perform as one who had worked hard, tried to do his best, and offered a candid approach to advise and support students with special needs, no matter what job I held or institution I served. You might say I won more games than I lost and characterize myself as being a singles and doubles hitter. I won the game of success, but I will always feel a spiritual nudge to remind me of my imperfections and shortcomings, and recognize that there is more to being successful than what is perceived by the symbols we use to describe our contributions.

You cannot always hit the ball out of the park, but you can rise above the fray and make a positive difference in the lives of others. Returning now to that batter in the ninth inning mentioned above, his name was Buster Posey and he hit a two-run double to win the game for the Giants that day. So, can you guess if this game was fact or fiction? What is fact is that later that year, in November 2010, the San Francisco Giants became World Series Champions by beating the Texas Rangers, winning four out of five games. I never thought I would live to witness the Giants win their first World Series championship in fifty-six years—or for us locals, fifty-two years after the Giants moved from New York City to San Francisco in 1958.

I played the game of life honestly and with a great deal of effort. When I was under the line of fire, I stood the course and met many of my challenges. I scored the final run of the game and I walked away feeling mostly very good about myself.

As I offered a final farewell to Napa Valley College and to all the other locations where I worked over a thirty-seven-year period, I attended commencement ceremonies, which for me were always the high moment of the academic year, a special moment to be proud of, not only for the students but for myself as well.

NVC's commencement is on the Friday of Memorial Day weekend. Faculty always brought their robes and tassels to the administration building and helped each other put on this traditional attire. The robes were dark but the hoods and tassels were colorful. Like the students marching into the auditorium to receive their degrees,

I always felt elated to wear the academic attire that represented my accomplishments. It was an honor and a privilege to walk with this fraternity of professionals who gave their all to instruct and support students. Walking in perfect formation in advance of the graduating students, the sounds of the Pomp and Circumstance march were calling us forward to take our seats and celebrate and honor our deserving students. As celebrities are introduced, speeches given, and degrees and certificates presented, we are hopeful these graduates will be successful in today's world. Having sat through countless commencement ceremonies, I am convinced the significance of all of these celebrations is to remind us of our roots and what we will do to construct new foundations to make a difference for the good of all society.

So, as the curtain came down to close out my long career, I believe I made a difference in helping people move forward in their lives. My former clients and students deserve most of the credit for their progress. My job was to open the door just a little bit wider so they could walk through. When a situation was not working out for me or my clients, I always tried to take a step back and reflect upon what I could have done differently. I loved my work, and once I reached a point where I believed I really had something to offer people, I was able to sail my ship with minimal turbulence.

I looked forward to my retirement years, where I hoped to experience new challenges and enjoy more of life's special moments without the daily pressures of performing on the job. I would not miss attending countless staff meetings or writing long narrative reports. What I would miss was working with colleagues who were helpful when I needed to resolve an issue. I will always remember the Workability III program staff and their team approach to assist students with academic and social challenges. I found it especially rewarding when once or twice a year Catherine, our program manager, gave us a full day away from the office to enjoy off-campus activities related to culture or education. We did things like visit museums, enjoy lunch at exotic restaurants, or hike in beautiful areas. Like summer camp at Enchanted Hills, Napa Valley College was a special venue with the fondest of memories.

Chapter 14

Retirement: The Golden Years

At the outset of my retirement, I learned quickly that I had a great deal of time on my hands. My family had thrown a retirement party for me outdoors at my mother's home. It was a wonderful way to close the chapter on my formal work life and share special moments with family, friends from Napa Valley College, and people I had known for over fifty years. And it was magnificent to wake up on weekday mornings and not have to rush off to deal with a work environment.

But I had decided to take on my retirement years with optimism and the determination to experience and learn new things every day. The first exciting event was climbing aboard a cruise ship to Alaska. I was born with the travel bug and vividly recall my excitement at boarding this magnificent ship. I had no idea what to expect. I shared a stateroom with my cruise-loving friends Rick and Lucy. We began each day by climbing the many stairs to the ship's mini-gymnasium, where we pumped iron and rode stationary bikes, hoping to burn more calories than we would acquire from the tasty cuisine on the ten-day trip. Dinner was a gourmet heaven. Every food imaginable was placed before us with elegance fit for a king. The fish and meat dishes were outstanding, but dessert was another world and beyond description.

I also learned how relaxing it is to lie on the deck in a lounge chair, listening to the ship ride the endless waves. The air was always fresh and cool, and the view of the horizon remained the same as we traveled. I enjoyed the bands and dancers and singers, but the high point was exiting the ship and becoming a tourist in our primary ports of call. Highlights were visiting a salmon hatchery and touring a totem pole factory in Skagway, observing a famed glacier in Juno, and attending an old West musical show in Ketchikan. On the way home from Alaska, the ship is required to put ashore at an international port, and we spent about four hours on a walking tour of Victoria, British Columbia. This city is beautiful, though I would have enjoyed it more had it been sunny instead of overcast and raining. On most cruises, the time spent in port cities is never long enough to gain an understanding of the culture and history. Even so, this first of my several cruise experiences was great.

During most of the first few months after retirement, I lived in San Mateo taking care of my eighty-nine-year-old mother, who was beginning to require more physical support. I was also spending time in Carson City, helping my family ease the transition of dealing with a house fire that had severely damaged our home and required them to stay in a rental for six months. Living in the house at the time were Eileen, our daughter Carolyn and her two sons Keegan and Cullen, and our son Michael.

    At the time of retirement, my options had included returning to Carson City and living with Eileen and our extended family. However, I did not want to be dependent upon others to get around. Carson City is a nice place to live, but there is minimal public transportation and the culture is very different from what I am accustomed to in the Bay Area. Also, my relationship with Eileen had changed over time. There were many years where I had supported my family by working away from home, and saw them only on long weekends and holidays. Eileen had had to take on full responsibility for caring for the kids during my absence. As we ventured apart, our interests and priorities changed to some degree. At times disappointment and friction occurred. Ultimately, I had to decide whether I wanted to remain as a full-time partner in the relationship. This decision was made more difficult when Eileen and I assumed full-time guardianship of two grandsons, Cullen and Keegan, when our daughter Carolyn was killed in a car accident just a year and a half after my retirement, on our thirty-fifth wedding anniversary.

Eileen and I still respect and care for each other. Our long marriage and love for each other produced five wonderful children who have given us, to date, six grandchildren. I have enjoyed the responsibilities of fatherhood, trying to be the best father I could, and suffering quietly when my children's lives were challenged with disappointments and sadness. The love of family brings Eileen and me together to rejoice in the goodness in what is before us, faulting no one in these personal and unique relationships. The rhythm of the peaks and valleys of life sustains us, no matter how difficult the frustrations. So, as time moves forward, I find myself still wanting to support Eileen emotionally and financially, and help out when I can to care for my two grandsons.

Even now, during her retirement years, my sister-in-law Terry continues to be there for all of us with her supporting ways and gestures of kindness. Terry strives to add to everyone's quality of life by ensuring that the grandchildren have a ride to school or taking them to a dentist or doctor's appointment when their mother or grandmother is occupied. Terry is a down-to-earth person who loves hiking, reading books, and adding her wisdom to family discussions.

Although I didn't have a daily job to go to, retirement did not slow me down when I returned from the cruise in early September 2010. There would be times in the coming years when the wanderlust bug took over, and I found myself taking the train to San Antonio, Texas;

Washington D.C.; and Holland, Michigan, among other places. I used to love getting on a plane and visiting a city like New York or Washington D.C. But one day on a flight to Chicago, the plane suddenly dropped hundreds of feet and shook violently. Since then the train has been my preferred mode of travel.

On a train you are able to relax, read or listen to a good book, make new acquaintances, and enjoy meals in the dining car, often with people you don't know but who are friendly and inquisitive and enjoy sharing parts of their lives over a glass of wine or an Angus steak with mashed potatoes. Later, you crawl into bed in your roomette, where you hear and feel the sound and rhythm of the train wheels on the tracks. The continuous motion and the excellent shock absorber system built into the passenger car quickly put you to sleep as you move toward your destination.

As I sat in the vista car or looked through my roomette window, I was treated to views of the Rocky and Sierra Nevada snow-capped mountains, the green farmlands of the Midwest, or the Pacific Ocean. I feel fortunate to witness these beautiful landscapes from inside one of mankind's great inventions.

The stops along the way allow the opportunity to get off the train and walk around the local station and its surroundings. In Tucson, Arizona, for example, you are immediately captivated by the ornate dark wood paneling on the walls and the decorative old-fashioned white tile floor that was probably installed near the start of the twentieth century. A stop in Oregon to refuel and pick up passengers and supplies allows time to take a brief jog among your fellow travelers as they mingle and enjoy the fresh Oregon air.

I feel gratitude and support for the Red Cap personnel who work at most Amtrak stations in the U.S. They have the endless responsibility of meeting incoming and outgoing passengers and helping to get them and their luggage to or from a train, the VIP lounge, or the exit. Most of these workers are courteous and helpful to travelers with disabilities or the elderly who need special assistance. Tipping Red Cap porters for their service is always appreciated. Arriving at the larger railroad stations like Chicago, Los Angeles, Portland, Denver, and Washington D.C., you are soon swept up in the busyness of a train travel hub. People are walking and running to make their train. Food aromas from nearby restaurants are in the air, and there are small boutiques for shopping. Amtrak personnel in these facilities are usually friendly, accommodating, and willing to answer questions. The ornate beauty and atmosphere of Union Station in D.C. is one of my favorites. Towering dome ceilings capture your attention, as do beautiful tile floors in designs laid out over a hundred years ago. The diverse sounds of people coming and going are magnified by the openness of the space inside the station. I hope passenger train travel never disappears due to modern technology. There are delays with train travel, but an unexpected stoppage allows a traveler to take time for reflection and relaxation. Train travel is a nineteenth century marvel and a twenty-first century curiosity.

On the train, I have encountered numerous people who had stories to tell and who listened to mine. I was fortunate to meet Crystal, for example, a young woman traveling from Wisconsin to a new job in Northern California. The conversation flowed easily and she shared her life story, her uncertainty at age twenty-five, and her search for stability and purpose. She even took out her guitar and sang me a song she'd composed. I was amazed that she spoke so openly to me, a man in his seventies, and I felt enriched and revitalized as I listened. My six-hour trip seemed much shorter than usual, and we still text one another now and then to keep up with our lives.

A different kind of encounter occurred in the summer of 2004 when I was traveling with my son Michael from Reno, Nevada to

Denver, Colorado. We were in coach, seated near the back of the car for the disabled and seniors who required special accommodations. Our ride on the California Zephyr, through the beautiful Sierra Nevada and Rocky Mountain regions was going along just fine until nightfall, when a man with a louder than normal voice, sitting at the front of the car, began a tirade of epithets and negative comments about Black people and others from diverse backgrounds. I gathered from his conversation that he was affiliated with some kind of church. His vestments were colorful, and you could easily see them because he was a large fellow. I assumed he was clergy.

As he continued his castigations, I grew more and more angry. Why should I have to listen to this bigot? I asked myself if I should say something so he would stop belittling our brothers and sisters of a different skin color or culture. I was upset, too, because in my view it was hypocritical for a man of the cloth to talk in this way.

As he intensified his remarks, his voice was more noticeable and he repeated the same things again and again. I noticed that most of the other passengers in the car had grown very quiet. I finally stood up, walked to his seat and told him to cease his biased remarks. I also offered my two cents about how wrong he was. After a couple of attempted responses, he grew frustrated, packed up his belongings, and left the car. Michael was laughing from his seat in the back and was in full support of my response. He could not believe I had challenged this religious person. In other words, Michael saw a different side of his dad.

My train travels after retirement took me on memorable trips to visit family and friends, as well as to tour the Gettysburg battlefield, visit the Holocaust Museum in Washington D.C., and spend a full exciting day in New Orleans. In September 2017, I signed up with the Road Scholar Program and spent five days touring Boston and witnessing a dream come true when I attended a Boston Red Sox game at Fenway Park. In addition, I went to Hyde Park, the home of Franklin D. Roosevelt in New York. During the three days I was there, I received the red carpet treatment and a memorable tour of the entire estate.

This latter adventure was made possible because since 2016 I have volunteered as a docent with the USS Potomac, FDR's yacht in the San Francisco Bay Area. This came about after I heard John Miller, the San Francisco Giants broadcaster, speak on the radio about how much he'd enjoyed a Bay voyage on the Potomac. I called the executive director of the Potomac Association, who offered me a tour of the yacht. I soon became a docent providing dockside and Bay tours for tourists, students, and others interested in the Roosevelt legacy. The Hyde Park museum and its surrounding estate was a beautiful and welcoming place. The green hillsides and tree-lined paths reminded me of a national park. The simplicity and lack of pretense at Springwood, Roosevelt's main residence, and Top Cottage, his personal retreat abode, confirmed my opinion that even though FDR came from wealth, his heart was in helping and supporting the common person to improve upon their life struggles.

As my retirement years unfolded, I took on volunteer work for organizations that meant a lot to me and part-time jobs that gave me pleasure. I remember attending my first symphony in the spring of 1958 at Berkeley High School. At that time, the San Francisco Symphony scheduled young people's concerts throughout the Bay Area. The School for the Blind had arranged for twenty-five of us kids to attend the concerts. We always sat near the front row. I was captivated by the wonderful sounds of the violins and the violas. When all four sections of the orchestra came together, the sounds were terrific. I was also impressed by the conductor, who prior to a particular piece, would speak to us, giving background about the composer and the piece to be played. As an adult, I became a regular symphony goer whenever I had the time and money.

So, when I retired, I wanted to get involved with the San Francisco Symphony to help this wonderful organization endure. I eventually served as a docent for about three years with the Upper Peninsula League, whose mission is to raise funds for the Symphony as well as offer students and seniors opportunities to attend concerts at Davies Hall. In that capacity, I made presentations to elementary and junior high school students who were scheduled to attend a young people's concert. I oriented the students to the instrumental sections of the orchestra, reviewed the Symphony's history, talked about the composers, and played music they would hear on the day of the concert, to get their reaction. For several years, in the spring, I also took seniors to the Symphony for a special trip, guiding the group onto the bus, distributing box lunches, providing tickets, and orienting them to the event once we arrived at the Hall. On one occasion, the bus driver, who must have been inebriated, drove the bus under an underpass and got stuck. I was the one who called for help and arranged for the seniors to get home.

It is always a memorable moment when I walk into Davies Hall in San Francisco and take my seat in anticipation of the performance. I look up to see the acoustical sound adjusters that hang down from the top of the hall. I am cognizant that at capacity, 2,700 other people will also be witnessing this musical experience. As the time comes near for the conductor to take center stage, the musicians have completed their warmup activities, and the concert master offers final tuning notes along with the oboe player. The Hall darkens except for the stage lighting, the conductor appears, and the concert begins. I don't always enjoy every piece of music on the program, but I do like, as I listen, to project myself into the mind of the composers as they created the music for a special occasion, historical event, or religious celebration.

The most exciting of my retirement positions, however, is that I landed a position with the San Francisco Giants. This was like a dream come true . . .

Chapter 15

A Coveted Job and the Opportunity of a Lifetime

When I returned from the cruise in early September of 2010, I was following the exploits of the San Francisco Giants as they were trying to win the National League Western Division Pennant. Baseball has always been a second love of mine. In particular, I have been an avid fan of the Giants since they arrived in San Francisco in 1958. The Giants have a history of exciting times where they won and lost close games, made good and bad plays, signed superstar players, and ultimately became World Series Champions within a five-year period by winning in 2010, 2012, and 2014.

I attended my first major league game with my cousin Sylvia in 1959 at the old Seal Stadium, the Giants' ballpark for two years after they arrived in San Francisco from New York, before they moved to Candlestick Park in 1960. The Giants happened to win that day, and I went home a happy camper. After retiring, I decided I wanted to become part of this world class organization. I contacted the Giants' Guest Services department and scheduled an informational interview with Alexis Lustbader, who coordinated the stadium tours program. She was willing to consider me for a job in line management, which falls under the broad classification of usher and includes diverse jobs around the stadium.

Our meeting went well, but a long time elapsed before I received a job application, because Alexis had moved to a different position. Some months later I was invited to an interview. I was so excited I probably slept little the night before. Applicants were interviewed individually by an HR employee, then in a groups of four by two or three Giants personnel. I thought my interview went well and felt optimistic that I might be working for the team I'd rooted for over 50 years. However, it was months before I was contacted. Finally, in March 2014 I was invited to a training session at the ballpark. My dream of being affiliated with the Giants had become a reality.

A sidebar to this story is that one of my employment references was my neighbor, Jeff Kuiper, whose brother is Duane Kuiper, a primary announcer for the Giants. Jeff provided technical support during games. I will never know if this reference influenced the job offer. Even so, I felt that the way I articulated my skills and abilities for the position had been an influence as well.

The training was a four-hour orientation about everything related to the San Francisco Giants organization. You learn the rules of the game—not baseball, but what you as an employee can and cannot do. You cannot smoke on the premises. You cannot purchase food at vending operations during the game. You must wear a uniform. If you do not have your badge with you when you report at the gate, you are sent home.

My job as a line manager is to greet people, answer their questions, and make sure they are lined up according to regulations for crowd control. During the game, I often direct people to the ticket office, restaurants, and the Guest Services offices where people can store strollers and obtain "first-ever" game certificates—a free souvenir that shows the name and date of a child's first Giants game. Guest Services also provides wheelchairs for those who need them to get around the ballpark.

So, there I was on the first day of the Giants home season, walking into the stadium as a new employee for this historical sports franchise. I was astonished to find it takes approximately 1,800 employees to manage stadium operations during a nine-inning baseball game. In the Guest Services department alone, four to five hundred employees support the incoming crowds at every game.

As I walked from my locker through the inside of the stadium to my assigned position at the Marina gate, I would pass uniformed employees covering security, janitorial, food services, waste management, and IT tasks. Diverse aromas from food vendors and specialty restaurants around the park would whet my appetite, and I longed for a crab sandwich or a cold beer.

Before each game starts, a few of us convene underneath the center field bleachers to chat and await the possibility of a batting practice ball or two coming through the aisle opening to grab as a souvenir. Those of us lucky enough to grab a ball usually give it away to a child or fan with special needs. As our conversations continued, I heard the balls hit the bat and wondered with each sound if that was the one ball that would fly over the centerfield fence and roll down the gangway to a Guest Services recipient. These pre-game activities build excitement and anticipation for the first pitch. What a moment it is when fans stand for the National Anthem and applaud the players as they take their position to begin the game. This is baseball, and I have experienced the game as a fan and an employee.

When I was working in the Seal Plaza elevator at Oracle Park, I was fortunate enough to receive one of those pre-game practice balls that rolled under the bleachers. The elevator goes up and down only one story, and the ride takes only fifteen seconds. This does not give the elevator operator much time to engage people in conversation. However, I happened to be talking to a woman named Brenda and her twelve-year-old grandson, Seth. They were from San Jose and looked forward to watching the Giants win. "Have you ever caught a baseball at a game?" I asked. "No, but Seth always gives it a try," Brenda said. "Would you like to have a baseball?" I asked Seth. I had the ball in my locker. I handed Brenda my business card and in a few days shipped her the ball and other baseball items. Brenda confirmed that she would forward the ball to Seth.

In that short fifteen seconds, I had perceived Seth as a fine young man focused on doing good things in life. It was just an impression I had. I may never see Seth again, but that moment of sharing and exchanging a few words with strangers took no effort and was meaningful, and barriers between people or our abilities never entered the equation.

At Oracle Park (the stadium's current name), I determine my own work schedule. We must work at least thirty out of eighty-one games a year to retain our jobs. I work only at home games, between five and six hours per game. To receive a paid lunch hour, we must work beyond the minimum four hours. I usually work fifty to fifty-five games a year, including commencement ceremonies and concerts. The Giants offer their stadium for these events, under Giant Enterprises. They count as games if attendance is over ten thousand. If I work over fifty-one games, my salary increases the next year. Every year, I try to work the San Francisco State University commencement.

I work most often at the Marina gate, offering information and support to customers as they enter the stadium. The Marina gate is a preferred place to work because most fans enter the park via the other gates. At this gate, I am treated to wonderful views of the Bay and have witnessed special musical presentations performed nearby. It has also been satisfying to work at other jobs in the bleacher and arcade areas, and in the garden area between restaurants and a bar. After a few innings, fans get louder and sometimes start sitting on plants and leaving their food containers and plates on top of the stands housing the plants. We pick up the items and put them into the proper receptacles. I also enjoy working on the second level, monitoring young children playing on the vintage cable car in center field. On occasion I support another staff person to monitor people using the elevator that accesses the private, exclusive Gotham Club restaurant and bar.

The work at any stadium location is not difficult. We just have to remember one important mandate, which is to always treat the paying customer with respect and do everything possible to make their experience at the ballpark memorable enough so they want to return. The point is not to give in to people who are rude and disrespectful, but to maintain professionalism and an objective approach toward resolving an issue.

Although I am able to anticipate many questions fans ask, I am always striving to learn as much more as I can about the stadium that will be helpful to pass along. I especially enjoy working in the bleacher section of the ballpark. Yes, it would be nice to work in the Gotham Club area, or handle the demands of the rich and famous as they view games from the luxury suites, but where I am assigned most often has enabled me to appreciate the diversity of people who file into the ballpark. Most fans are kind, pleasant, and a delight to serve.

The Giants should be commended for their conscientious efforts to hire not only the blind and visually impaired but also many other physically impaired individuals. I have noticed, however, management's reluctance to consider people with disabilities for certain jobs in which they could perform the essential tasks. For example, I am disappointed when I am overlooked time and again for the job of handing out items during promotional giveaway days. Giveaway days are fun, and all an employee has to do is put their hand into a box and pull out a promotional item like a bobble head or t-shirt. I have done this job only once or twice in six years. I believe the perception is that a non-sighted person can't do this job well. However, I remain optimistic.

Another positive outcome is that I have developed a number of friendships and was awarded my five-year pin as a Giants employee earning the job title "Usher."

Again, as of this writing, as I stand at Oracle Park I am reminded of the special moments that occur when we hear the famous words "play ball" spoken by a young child over the public address system before the first batter comes to the plate. Then, we will come to the moment of the seventh inning stretch and join in singing "Take Me Out to the Ball Game," a ritual that reminds us of the history of this wonderful game. It has been my good fortune to attend Giants games in all three of their stadiums, beginning at Seal Stadium, moving to Candlestick Park, and finally AT&T Park in 2000. When I'm not working and attend a game as a fan, maybe two or three times a year, I always appreciate the opportunity to sit in Section 312, directly behind home plate on the view level of the ballpark. The views of the Bay and surrounding city are spectacular. I feel like I'm sitting on top of the field viewing the game. I can never see all of the action due to my visual impairment, but just being there and feeling and hearing the fans' enthusiasm excites me, especially when my team is winning. My transistor radio is always at my ear, which allows me to never miss a beat as the game progresses.

One of the greatest baseball moments of my life occurred around the first of November in 2014 when I and other Guest Services staff and key Giants' personnel had the honor of accompanying the ball club in their World Series victory parade down Market Street and ending at City Hall. As I walked along Market Street, tears rolled down my face as the crowd cheered in celebration. We were all waving our orange and black commemorative rally rags, which look like small towels with the Giants logo on them. Fans wave the towel when the team is scoring runs or when the pitcher strikes out an opposing player at a crucial point in the game. As I walked, I happened to hear a young bystander ask if she could have one of the towels. Without thinking much about it, I walked over to the crowd barrier and gave her my piece-of-history rally rag. I could not see her face, but I heard the appreciation in her voice as she said thank you.

They say baseball is a game of inches between winning and losing. I always feel like a winner when I enter Oracle Park because of my great love for the Giants and because there is never a dull moment in witnessing games from inside this facility. I was attending the game over fifty years ago when Willie Mays and Orlando Cepeda were hitting home runs out of Seal Stadium and Candlestick Park. I witnessed outstanding pitching performances by Gaylord Perry and Juan Marichal. In August 2010, I was sitting with my daughter Jenny in the upper deck as Matt Cane pitched a two to zero shutout against the hated Los Angeles Dodgers, pushing the Giants one game closer to winning the Western Division Pennant and subsequently the World Series. So, the game of baseball is America's favorite pastime, and when our home team players run the bases and score a run, we are treated to one of those special moments in life where our spirits are high and nothing else matters. As we exit the ballpark after the game, we return to our homes fully satisfied with the outcome and at times simultaneously contemplating if they can win another game the next day.

The game of baseball offers many metaphors for reflection. My favorite moment is when a young child announces "Play ball" to the stadium crowd before the game. Beyond the game itself, wins and losses do not matter. Strikeouts are significant, but in the long run they urge players to try harder. As fans, we learn to cheer for good and bad plays, remembering the moments with great satisfaction or critical sarcasm. These situations can be applied to our daily lives, instilling in us that baseball is a team sport no matter what the results indicate. Baseball teaches us about life and how we can become better people. If we play ball well in life, we are assured the outcome will be beneficial for all concerned.

In addition to working for the Giants, applying for and accepting a part time job with the Golden State Warriors at the new Chase Center in San Francisco is not something I thought would ever happen. The Chase Center opened in August 2019. This multipurpose venue is on an eleven-acre site overlooking the San Francisco Bay in the Mission Bay section of the city. This facility, built at a cost of 1 billion 400 million dollars, is not only home to the Warriors but also offers concert performances by famous entertainers and accommodates conventions and other civic enterprises. Two of my colleagues at Oracle Park had been hired at the Center and kept taunting me to apply. They believed I would enjoy the challenge and add to the team spirit atmosphere that exemplifies the current management philosophy.

I spent weeks procrastinating and finally submitted an application in October 2019. I had to depend upon my neighbors Jeff and Tim and my colleague Steve to help me complete the many HR forms and application documents online. The screen reader (JAWS) does not always allow a blind consumer to access online documents. I had to bite my tongue and graciously accept their help and tell myself that at times I must accept support from others when the issue is beyond my grasp. I now find myself in a new environment facing new challenges and meeting new people.

My job at the Chase Center is in Guest Experience and involves assisting customers and fans at the arena. Mostly, I answer questions that pertain to where is my seat, what kind of food is available for someone who enjoys barbecued chicken, and where is the box office so I can upgrade my tickets. I work mostly at the information kiosk on the third level. We help hundreds of people there every evening.

Like the Giants' operation, we give out first-game certificates to fans, hand out sensory bags for persons who need earplugs and other devices to handle loud noises, and deal with other issues. I have had to memorize the location of portals and sections so I can quickly address people's questions. There are many bars and clubs in the arena and I have learned where they are and how they accommodate fans. The staff at the Chase Center seems ahead of the game when it comes to accommodating my particular needs. When I first started working there, night after night I would be standing along the east side corridor and hardly interacting with customers. The time went by very slowly. When I approached the manager of Guest Experience, she moved me to the kiosk, where I now enjoy myself because I am always busy.

My biggest challenge was learning how to get around this beautiful facility with its many corridors, sections, portals, restaurants, and clubs. The ADA coordinator (a Chase Center employee) has agreed to contact the LightHouse for the Blind to develop a Brailled map that would allow me identify the location of specific places in the arena, as do sighted employees who use printed maps to direct guests. I would have to rely on my memory by studying the map independently on my own. This will be a trial and error process, and it might not be practical. But we are taking advantage of this accommodation and will try it.

I am impressed that my coworkers are gracious and willing to answer my questions and that management strives to address employee issues promptly. For example, it was apparent from the start that I would need help recording my in and out time on the time clock. A visually impaired person cannot access the time clock because the printed directions on the screen are very small. So, before I could sign in or out, I had to ask a friend or stranger to help me through the process by giving them my employee number. After I spoke with management about this, HR suggested as an accommodation that I just submit the date, time, and hours worked to the intake manager of operations who is responsible for scheduling. This has worked well.

Working at the Chase Center is another example of extending myself into unexpected opportunities that come my way and that are enriching my life in retirement.

Chapter 16

My Family: A Tribute

My mother was not thrilled to have me return home to live with her when I retired. At the outset, she didn't want me to handle household chores such as cooking, cleaning, and using the washer and dryer. She seemed to have forgotten that for twenty years I had lived on my own and knew how to take care of myself. "Where are you going? When will you be back?" she would ask. "How are you getting to San Francisco?" "Be careful not to get hit by a car." "Be sure and take the lint out of the dryer screen when you finish drying your clothes." Her view was that no matter how old you are, when it comes to skills of daily living, your disability means you will always need help.

She has never fully accepted that I am an adult and can make viable decisions without asking her for approval. As her firstborn and blind, I'm sure she was still in the habit of trying to keep me safe. Also, even at her advanced age, she wanted to control and monitor what her children were doing. This is perhaps a natural instinct mothers have for their offspring. But the tension in the house was high.

As time went on, however, my mother seemed to accept and appreciate my presence. She started to enjoy that I could cook meals for both of us (especially my carrot soup) and operate the washer and dryer without her help. She began to see me as a resource who could help her.

When I first moved in with her at retirement, she was eighty-nine. She was still active, lunching with her golfing friends, and driving in her car to shop for groceries and get her hair done every Friday morning. Her spirits were high, and she thrived on going about her business in a positive way.

In January of 2019, as I was writing this book, the situation drastically changed. My mother fainted in the family room as my sister Marianne was attempting to get her back in her chair. An ambulance took her to the hospital, where she was diagnosed with lung clots that could end her life at any time. She began receiving 24-hour care at home and blood thinners to promote circulation. She is in good spirits, however, and turned one hundred in August 2021.

As she became less able to take of herself over the years, I would help her in the morning to get out of bed and to the bathroom, and then I prepared her breakfast. I helped her with other meals and cooked her dinner. In the evening, I helped her dress for bed and get into bed. There were moments when I had trouble getting her clothes off, or she fell over me while I was taking off her shoes. There were times when I sat outside her bathroom door, awaiting her request to assist her from the bathroom. There were also cries and calls for help during the wee hours of the night.

This daily routine began to adversely affect me. But eventually it dawned on me that through my mother's aging issues, I was gaining tolerance and understanding. I had to learn patience and put her needs before my own. I learned how to become a more effective support person for her. So, even though we had hired part-time caregivers prior to the episode in 2019, I was often on my own in trying to assist her. Even though it was difficult to maintain patience and understanding, the bottom line is that my mother has always come first with respect to her care and her increasing needs.

During these last three years, since January 2019, I no longer have had to get up in the middle of the night and respond to her calling out for support. I have not had to call the fire department or knock on a neighbor's door to help get her off the floor when she fell out of bed. I want her to live as long as she can, with some semblance of having quality of life. She has lived her life to the fullest and now has to endure ongoing care for the many needs she was once able to perform for herself. I have to balance my love for my mother with doing as much as I can to ensure she has quality care in her final days. My mother always appears to look well, given her skin color and facial expressions, but cognitively she is unable to function in ways that typify who she is and was. This weighs on me and I try to be objective and remind myself that I might be in her shoes some day and would appreciate kind gestures from family members, caregivers, and friends.

When I become frustrated with my mother, I remind myself what a special mother she has been for me and my brother, Paul, and our sister, Marianne. I will never forget how she accompanied me weekly and sat with me when I was having x-rays for countless childhood earaches. She took me to many medical and eye exam appointments. She drove on weekends to pick me up from the School for the Blind. Once, I could not go home for the weekend because I had been exposed to measles. She came to visit me in the school infirmary.

My mother was an only child and grew up in a protected world, but was able to flourish in a changing society through her wonderful personality and ability to acquire good friends and enjoy a full life with her husband. She grew up in Vallejo, California and met my father, Sam, in San Francisco at Heald Business College. Her ancestors migrated to the US from England and Ireland, and my father's family from Italy. Grandma Dana (born Houghton) had a tremendous influence on me.

My mother has witnessed her grandchildren grow into adulthood and have children of their own. Her longevity has allowed her to witness multiple changes in the way technology enables us to live our lives. Even as she is bedridden, I am amazed when she comments on how nicely I am dressed or offers me good wishes as I'm on my way out the door. She is still positive about life and warmly welcomes friends and family to her bedside. So, to Mom I say thanks for these memories, and I am grateful to you for being my mother and for being there to encourage and support me throughout my life. The road has not always been smooth between us, but I have learned to be more tolerant and forgiving.

On August 11, 2018, soon after I had started writing this book, my brother, Paul Martin Dana, passed away suddenly in his home. He was about to take his young dog Caley for a walk. Paul was seventy-one, with a bright future still ahead. The cause of death was probably a heart attack or stroke, though we never received a definitive report.

The sudden loss of my brother gave me many moments to pause and think about life in general and how the grieving process impacts our ability to move on with our lives. The shock of his death and the reality that we would never speak again were disheartening. We were about to celebrate my mother's 97th birthday with a dinner at her home. Marianne was cooking dinner when Paul's wife, Judy, called with the news.

Paul was active even at the age of seventy-one. He swam at the Elks Lodge daily. He was an avid fisherman and played an occasional game of golf. He had worked as a health inspector for the county and was loved and respected by his coworkers. What I miss most about my brother is our conversations about Bay Area sports: the Giants, the Forty-niners, and the Golden State Warriors. When I needed to go out of town, Paul was always available to take me to the train or

BART station. We were not the closest brothers, but we respected one another and got along most of the time. I am only three years older than Paul, but he always seemed to be the older sibling, since he was the first of us to begin dating and because he began driving at sixteen. When we lose a loved one, our hearts are broken and sometimes our coping mechanisms are challenged as we attempt to move on with our lives.

Marianne was the youngest child. As my parents' only daughter, she was spoiled by our father and tormented occasionally by her two older brothers. Marianne became an English teacher and later a junior high and high school art teacher. Her daughter Emily is an occupational therapist. Marianne goes to baseball games with me and is always excited when I invite her to symphonies and concerts. I will never forget the support Marianne extended to me, Eileen, and my children, when my daughter Carolyn died. Marianne also single handedly coordinated my retirement party. I deeply love and respect Marianne, even though I wish she would learn to relax in those moments where her frustrations impede her happiness. As we moved through the period of mourning our brother, we learned to put aside our personal reactions and judgments and arrange for the care and support of our mother.

All my life, my mother actively supported my accomplishments and my efforts to excel in whatever I was doing, professionally or personally. At age sixty-three, while I was working in Napa, I trained to participate in my fourth marathon. Michael, a junior in high school, would run with me. My mother drove all the way from San Mateo to celebrate the event.

Carolyn drove Michael to Napa from Carson City, and he and I spent time running and eating lots of pasta the day before the race. We rose early on Sunday morning and were bussed to Calistoga, in north Napa County, where the race began. It was a cool morning, and the two of us ran together for a number of miles. Since Michael was the young buck, I encouraged him to run at his own speed and pace. He decided to run ahead and meet me at the finish line. Running a marathon requires training and endurance, as well as mental and psychological preparation, and on a 26.2 mile race, you learn very quickly to pace yourself. The strategy is to run a few miles, then walk for a moderate period, then begin running again. In three previous marathons, a friend or guide had accompanied me. After Michael ran ahead, I was on my own. I missed a turn and fell halfway down a small hill from the edge of the road.

I was not injured, but I learned to be careful of an obstacle such as the point where the blacktop road surface blends with the color of a raised curb at the edge of the road. I have no depth perception and could not see that the two surfaces of the same color were not on the same plane. I moved forward with a bit of hurt ego, but finished the marathon within the five-and-a-half-hour limit. My body was stiff and sore, and I could hardly walk. Michael approached me with the news that he had finished at the four-hour mark. We hugged and congratulated one another and had dinner that evening with Carolyn and Grandma Barbara (my mother). She would not have missed this opportunity to support my competitive sports activity and enjoy the company of whichever of her grandchildren were present.

And running a marathon with Michael was a special moment. I love him with my whole heart and soul and am blessed to have such a loving son who exemplifies all that is good. I was almost forty-six when Michael was born, yet there is no generation gap between us. We love each other unconditionally, and when we're together we have a wonderful time sharing in the spirit of whatever the moment brings.

This tribute to the Dana family would not be complete without mention of the six grandchildren I have been blessed with, starting with Donovan, born in July 1999. He had to grow up fast given that his mother, Monica, and his father were dealing with relationship issues that led Donovan's upbringing to fall upon his grandmother, Eileen, and my children during some crucial years of his development. Donovan has grown into a tremendous adult, working as a manager in a food market and studying business skills in college, after briefly exploring work as an emergency technician and a firefighter. Donovan has a special spirit and I always enjoy our interactions. My only disappointment is that I can no longer beat him at arm wrestling.

Keegan and Cullen, my other two grandsons, arrived in this world in 2003 and 2007. They are living out their lives without the benefit of either parent being present. They were very young when their mother Carolyn passed away, and their father was not able to fully care for and support them. Most of the credit goes to their grandmother, Eileen, who has made many sacrifices to ensure these boys were raised in the spirit of love and with the means to endure life's challenges. Keegan is strong-willed and handsome and popular with girls. He is intelligent, compassionate, musically talented, and active in sports, but his grades are not consistent and he has social problems in school. The consensus is that many of his problems result from depression after his mother's death. Our entire family loves and supports Keegan as he receives counseling to help him gain confidence and make wise decisions. I always encourage him to take the high road in life, which involves putting forth effort to learn and grow from his mistakes.

Cullen's life path has been different, given that he is the younger brother and also dealing with cognitive issues that have impacted his learning abilities. He is a kind and pleasant boy who loves to receive hugs. He enjoys dancing to loud music and busies himself by playing with animated toys such as model cars, Legos, and power water guns, and video games with his best friend. One of my favorite activities with Cullen is to ride bikes and take him bowling. At age eleven he was enrolled in a Montessori school, where students learn concepts at a gradual pace and take part in diverse learning opportunities such as caring for farm animals, cooking and preparing meals, and cleaning schoolrooms. Cullen is making progress in this new learning environment. Our hope is that he attains success and creates a quality-filled life for himself.

Recently Cullen and a close friend signed up to play basketball through a local recreation center. They relentlessly contributed to the success of the team by sharing the ball when it came to scoring points. Their contribution added to the team spirit and the two boys were honored at the final celebration meal at a local pizza parlor. Given that both boys had never played basketball before and had cognitive issues, they had performed beyond expectations. I believe this experience will go far to enhance their self-esteem.

I have had the good fortune to be given three beautiful granddaughters as well, all younger than my grandsons, but not by much. Shalleigh Eileen, Jenny's oldest daughter, was born in January 2009. Shalleigh is a special young lady who knows what she wants and when she wants it. She likes to ski and loves art. She is close to her cousin Cullen and a driving force who challenges him to play games with her. She is high-spirited and will do and try anything to win at board games and other competitive activities. She is fearless and determined and pursues life with enthusiasm and vigor. She constantly coaxes me to run around and play tag with her, a reminder that I fit the mold of an elderly grandpa. Shalleigh will make her mark in this world as a proactive and intelligent woman whose voice will be heard whether or not her input is requested.

Annabella Leigh is my second oldest granddaughter, born in 2011. Annabella is another spirited child born to Jenny and her husband, Christopher. Jenny works as a health systems analyst in an office where employees are allowed to bring their newborns to work.

Jenny used to tell me how her coworkers took turns carrying Annabella around the office when her mother was busy. I support such programs in the work setting, and assume Annabella's personality and self-confidence were influenced by being held and rocked as a baby by multiple people who worked with my daughter. Annabella has asserted to everyone around her that she loves her grandfather very much. "Grandpa, I will love you forever even when you die," she once declared. When I have not seen Annabella for a long time, she runs to me, jumping into my arms. When she was three, she was riding a four-wheel bicycle with other preschool children in a mini St. Patrick's Day parade around the neighborhood of her preschool. I was behind her, trying to help her maintain her balance on the bike. At one point she yelled out, "I am sure having the time of my life!" I am amazed at Annabella's rich vocabulary, beyond her age. My love for Annabella goes beyond description.

Bridget Marie was born in March of 2016. Even at three, she was an active and domineering little girl. She is very loving, but more times than not, she will tell you to go away. Bridget has a loud and proactive demeanor. She does not like to hear the word "no." When she does, she screams and yells and runs to find her father. Occasionally, Bridget will grab my hand and direct me to a nearby coffee table to encourage me to play puzzle games with her.

In my view, the family is the primary foundation of our lives. Our family interactions and experiences mold us into the people we become. We are nurtured, supported, loved, and disciplined by those around us who influence our very existence.

The family unit is an integral part of our development and support as we mature and grow into adulthood. It is our love for one another that enables us to forgive and try to love again. There are of course broken families full of dysfunction, anger and depression. Even though some people might believe that "families who pray together, stay together," it takes more than prayer to bring resolution and peace of mind to people in turmoil and despair.

I have loved and cherished my family members, even though with almost everyone I have had adverse and challenging moments that shook me to the core. Often enough, friction and anger subsided when heated arguments turned into constructive dialogue, once our egos got out of the way. We have to work on ourselves to forgive and move to some high ground that is mutually acceptable for those around us.

The Dana children, 1992. Standing: Monica, age 13; Carolyn, 12. Seated: Jenny, 10; Michael, 15 months; Laura, 6.

Tom and Jay Henderick. Jackson Hole, Wyoming, 2003.

Tom, his father Sam, his daughter Jenny, his brother Paul, his daughter Laura (seated), his mother Barbara. Christmas 2003.

Tom's father Sam, Tom's son Michael, Tom, Tom's grandson Donovan. June 2003.

Tom and daughter Laura, 2014.

Tom and Eileen with Monica, Jenny, and Carolyn, 1981.

Tom, Larry, and Jay, 2008.

Tom's granddaughter Shalleigh with son-in-law Christopher, 2009.

Tom and Eileen, wedding day, October 9, 1976.

Tom with his grandchildren. Back row: Donovan, Cullen, Keegan, Second row: Shalleigh, Annabella. Seated: Tom, Bridget. June 2022.

Chapter 17

The Psychology of Disability

One evening during a week-long visit with my dear friend Larry in Eureka in January of 2001, we decided to watch a video of Victor Borgia performing his comedy routines at the piano. Larry was laughing his head off, but my response was less than enthusiastic because I could not see Borgia's antics, which focused on gestures and body movement. At some point Larry realized why my reactions were so different from his. We discussed the situation, and since that day, when we are together Larry does not miss a beat in describing what is going on around us, whether we're looking at a painting in a museum, an item in a boutique, or a restaurant menu. Larry has mastered his fear of what to say or do around me and has become so comfortable that he rarely thinks about his visually impaired "brother" as someone with a disability. Before we met, he had no previous interaction with a visually impaired person. He has become a competent sighted guide.

A few years earlier, when I worked at Victor Valley College, I had the opportunity to teach a psychology course. Psychology is defined as "the scientific study of the human mind and its functions, especially those affecting behavior in a given context." The context I chose (then and now) was to identify the behaviors and attitudes between the marginalized and the rest of society. These are always in flux; they can change with every interaction and experience.

This "psychology of disability" is the context and foundation for embracing how we can make positive changes in our lives if we are open to modifying our attitudes as we learn to engage with those who, at first, look upon us differently.

Disabled folks are always on stage, viewed by others, accepted or unfairly judged, putting the onus on us to react in the most appropriate way we can, given the nature of our mental, physical, or sensory disability. If our audience does not like what they see in our performances in social settings, we will ultimately receive poor reviews and inconclusive reactions when they encounter us again.

People often ask me about my disability, and it's often a two-part question: "How did you become blind? And what can you tell me to help me better understand your predicament?" My response is short and sweet. I explain that I was born prematurely and was given too much oxygen in the incubator, which caused retinal issues resulting in partial blindness. I explain that my blindness is not a disability, but rather a sensory impairment that can be addressed by various accommodations and sighted-guide techniques that allow me to be independent and self-sufficient. I also emphasize that being visually impaired does not keep me from doing things like watching television, playing baseball, or going grocery shopping on my own. I just can't see the same things you see when you do those things, but I enjoy them in my own way.

My goal is to put the questioner at ease and convey a positive disposition throughout our interaction. I want the person to walk away feeling comfortable and confident enough that in a similar situation they will apply this awareness to someone else with a disability.

When I was presenting disability awareness training, my objective was always to make the subject interesting and to offer simulation activities so participants could experience certain disabilities first-hand. When a participant wears a blindfold and walks with a sighted guide around a confined area, the person being led almost immediately feels confusion, fear, and dependency. These simulations bring home the point that people do survive with a disability, but must use accommodations and training to help them. When we lose one of our primary senses, such as sight, it takes a long time to adjust.

I cannot tell you how many times people have taken my arm and almost dragged me across a busy intersection because they saw me using a white cane. These individuals mean well, but the visually disabled person must be assertive and ask the would-be helper to please let us take their arm at the elbow. This allows us to feel the movement of the other person's body as we cross the intersection together. In this manner, the disabled person maintains control of the situation. Once we step onto the opposite curb, we can express our gratitude and be on the way to our next destination.

In the interest of making it easier for disabled and non-disabled people to interact more successfully and with greater understanding, I offer the following tips.

If you're disabled, here are suggestions for interacting with the non-disabled.

1. Pay attention to your self-talk.

If the voice in your head is doubtful or self-critical, switch to more positive statements. For example, say things like this to yourself:

"I know I have something to offer in my interactions with others."

"I am not going to let my insecurities get in the way of interacting with peers or friends."

"As I engage with other people, my mind will be clear of negative thoughts about myself or my disability."

"I feel good about what the day will bring."

Though it's normal to feel uncertain or uncomfortable in unfamiliar social or work situations, focusing on the positive will help.

2. Make an effort to put your best foot forward in social or work situations.

Smile. Use an icebreaker to open the conversation, such as "What do you think of this weather?" or "How's the job going?" or "How have you been since we last talked?"

When you're relaxed, you're helping the other person forget about your disability for the moment or even beyond. You're simply two human beings having a conversation. You won't have to try to make a good impression because you'll come across as relaxed and natural. You'll be yourself. And you won't contribute to stereotypes of the disabled.

3. Be forthright about your functional limitations.

Let the person you're speaking with know what you can and cannot do given your disability. For example:

If you're blind and having a meal with a friend or a new colleague in a restaurant, you might say, "Would you mind reading the menu to me?"

If you're in a wheelchair, you might ask the non-disabled person to squat down or take a seat on a chair next to you, so you can converse more easily.

Being forthright about your functional limitations can be done in a way that acknowledges you need assistance, but shows you are not helpless.

4. Educate your listener about your disability by noting your successes even though you have had to adapt to achieve success.

Describing your positive experiences steers the listener's focus away from your disability. For example, if you're in a wheelchair and interviewing for a job, it would be prudent to mention that you get to work via public transportation or that you're licensed to drive your own vehicle.

You might share your work accomplishments, such as special projects, professional recognition or honors, or professional opportunities you've taken advantage of.

If you're blind and you want to ask a sighted person to dinner, the person might be uncomfortable due to your disability. You could say something like: "We've known each other for a while, and I'm wondering if you'd like to go to dinner this weekend. I know a good place in North Beach. I could meet you there, or I can come to your house and you can drive. Or we could meet and take the bus together." Give the other person options.

If you're interviewing for a job, know your accommodation needs and state them matter of factly. At the same time, talk about your abilities in a way that people forget you're disabled. Doing so shows you're creative. You're taking your marginalism and putting it on the back burner.

5. **Always trust that no matter what happens in your interactions with others, some good can come out of it.**

If you want to improve your communications with others, you must be willing to take that initial step and share a part of your humanness. If disabled people put themselves in the mainstream as proactive communicators, then we will expand our comfort zones and the comfort of family, friends, coworkers, and strangers on our life path.

If you're non-disabled, here are some guidelines for interacting with the disabled.

1. Be aware of the person first and the disability second.
Focus on the person as they are speaking with you, and give the person a chance to share something about themself with you.

2. Ask *how* and *what* questions.
If you are talking with a visually impaired person, you might ask:

"How do you get around without help from another person?"

"How do you read books or fill out forms like a voting ballot?"

"I see that you use a special cane for walking, and I'm curious about what happened to bring about this situation in your life."

If you know that a hearing impaired person enjoys music concerts, you might ask: "What is it you enjoy about attending music concerts?"

3. Check your assumptions about the disabled.

For example, if you believe a deaf person can only communicate through sign language, you might check out that assumption by asking, "Is signing the only way I will be able to communicate with you?"

If an interpreter is not present, you could have a tablet available so you and the hearing impaired person can write back and forth to one another. You might begin by writing a note on a card, asking "Can we communicate in writing?"

By asking questions about your perceptions and fears about people with disabilities, you will realize that many of your concerns are not as important as you imagined. Asking pertinent questions can ease your concerns. Ask questions that are realistic and come from your heart. In most cases, the disabled person will be able to allay your concerns.

If you're a good listener, your confidence about talking with a disabled person will be enhanced as a result of the experience.

4. Understand the rules of disability etiquette. Here are just a few examples.

When an interpreter is present in speaking with a deaf person, proper etiquette is that you look at the deaf person, not at the interpreter, during the conversation.

When you offer to help someone with a white cane cross the street, and they say yes, proper etiquette is to offer your arm, so the person can hold on to you as you cross the street. It is not appropriate for you to take the arm of the person you are helping. Allowing the blind person to take your arm enables them to retain their sense of direction and feel more in control of the situation. If you take them by the hand or the shoulder and start pushing them forward, they lose their sense of being in charge and may feel they are losing control of the situation. By taking your elbow, the blind person is more stable as you cross the street. When the sighted person moves or changes direction, the blind recipient is able to quickly adjust and move in unison with that person. Also, be respectful and listen carefully to what the blind person says. They may or may not want your help.

A non-disabled person should speak to a wheelchair-bound person at that person's physical level. The person in the chair might have trouble lifting their head up. Their body space is in that chair. Wheelchair etiquette is that you speak to the wheelchair-bound person at the level they are sitting.

Before you move a wheelchair, ask permission of the wheelchair user, and follow that person's directions.

In a restaurant, don't order for a non-sighted person without their permission.

5. Ask yourself if you hold a mental stereotype of a person's disability, based on something that happened in the past.

People have ingrained attitudes and assumptions about the disabled. Maybe it's something their parent said when they were a child, like "Look at that poor little girl who has to walk with crutches." Or, "I guess that blind beggar on the street corner can't make ends meet because he can't see." Or, "That mentally disabled young man sure talks loud. He has no manners."

Question the labels about the disabled that pop into your mind based on stereotypes. Remind yourself that the stereotype is not reality.

6. Keep in mind that every disabled person is unique.

As individuals, the disabled are as varied and unique as the non-disabled. Disabled people become scientists, movie stars, senators, professors, artists, athletes, and more. Disability affects people of every culture and race.

Individually, the disabled have different needs and values, but because they are a minority, the general population judges them differently. They are often looked upon as deficient, unable to care for themselves, and dependent on society to meet their every need. The Americans with Disabilities Act did not come about because our society had reached an overall acceptance of marginalized people. Rather, the law was necessary to give disabled persons access to the same things that are enjoyed and accessed without thought by the general population.

7. Think of the long-term benefits of a relationship with this person.

For example, if you are hiring a person with a disability, you will soon realize how dedicated and committed the person is to performing at a high level in your organization. In social relationships, there is much to be gained for both of you as you get to know each other.

Another situation worth mentioning is that many people with disabilities must depend on public or commercial transportation. The train has always gotten me where I wanted to go over long distances, and for me provides enjoyment and relaxation. Every one of us who does not drive must familiarize ourselves with local and regional transportation. Where I live in the San Francisco Bay Area, adequate public transportation is available, so I can go most places on my own without help from other people.

There is, of course, the downside of public transit, ranging from scheduling mix-ups to mechanical breakdowns to rude passengers and bus drivers. On the positive side, I have encountered train conductors and alert bus drivers who, observing my visual limitations, offered support to ensure I would get to the correct place in the terminal. My traveling experiences near and far have taught me to be assertive and never be afraid to ask for help.

I have a few rules when I travel that aim to cultivate a positive interaction. My first order of business is always to break the ice with the bus driver or conductor. I ask questions about how long they have been driving a bus or been a conductor. Then we might get into a discussion about their families or hobbies. I might ask how to get to a location after I leave the bus or train, or in transit, how to move through the train to get to the club car or snack bar. There might be safety features of the train and I'll receive an update from the conductor. Once, an Amtrak bus driver traveling from Sacramento to Carson City, Nevada offered to drop me off in front of my home. It was quite a sight and privilege to have a large bus drive through the narrow streets of my neighborhood and stop at my front door. Those were the good old days. This happened because I had spent a lot of time conversing with the driver. It may be impossible to get such special treatment in our current transportation systems, but the point is to be congenial in interacting with the people you encounter in your travels.

As I see it, our task as disabled persons is monumental but not impossible. We must envision ourselves as confident and capable individuals who can make a difference in society not because of our disabling conditions, but through our unique attributes and talents. This comes through developing self-confidence and taking steps to gain experience that helps resolve our doubts and fears about our limitations. We are fortunate that the ADA guarantees our right to education and employment. We need to move beyond the old medical model of disability, which looked at people with disabilities as a problem to fix through medicine and rehabilitation programs. Our destiny can be brighter if we decide that life with a disability can be fulfilling, and we proactively engage in life's challenges.

As I mentioned earlier, one aspect of "the psychology of disability" is that disabled folks are always on stage, viewed by others, accepted or unfairly judged, putting the onus on us to react in the most appropriate way we can.

There is the classic story of a five-year-old girl who approached a young man in a wheelchair waiting to pay for his groceries in a store. As the girl asked the man why he was using a wheelchair, her mother rushed up and yanked her daughter away from the man. Perhaps the mother had experienced an adverse situation in her own life, maybe as a child, regarding a person with a disability, and feared for her daughter's safety. Or, she might have been raised by parents who believed that physical impairments at birth are caused by the will of God and wanted to keep her daughter at a distance.

This politically incorrect reaction still happens. Despite passage of the ADA, plenty of ignorance and misunderstanding remain.

The obvious question is how will this young girl react the next time she comes in contact with a person with a disability—a wheelchair user or a person with a white cane or guide dog crossing the street? Also, it is disheartening not to include the person in the wheelchair in this interaction. He has feelings, too. If you saw this scene, how would you react? What could have been done to make the situation a positive one for all concerned?

It is also incumbent upon those of us with a disability to assess a situation and use the proper decorum if we are being put upon by a do-gooder or stranger. Imagine the example mentioned earlier, where a person with a white cane is waiting to cross the street. An individual approaches and politely asks if the person requires help crossing the street. When the visually impaired person acts ungrateful or tells the person to get lost, what does this do for achieving acceptance and understanding from people who are trying to be helpful?

If we are performing on the open stage of life, we have an obligation to be courteous and politely assert that we can master the intersection without help (if that is indeed our preference at that moment). As people with disabilities, we must be vigilant about how we behave in social situations, so people who do not know how to act around us can be reassured that it's okay to intervene the next time they see a person with a disability who might need some simple assistance. We must always take the high road in our efforts to have successful interactions with our non-disabled sisters and brothers. We must challenge ourselves to do our part, big or small, by putting the general public more at ease so they will come to accept our empowerment as contributing members of society. If by doing this we can modify attitudes and behavior, then breakthrough on their part will occur.

As a community college educator and academic counselor, it took me many years to realize that education is power. With a degree or a vocational certificate, many more opportunities become available for people with special needs. This became apparent in my own life and in observing the wonderful things that happened to my students when they began to experience success as they completed their degrees.

When I first met many of these students, they had doubts about their future, they struggled with parental attitudes of negativity toward higher education, and they were concerned that their disability would impede their progress in the educational setting. The culmination of their academic efforts occurred when they walked on stage at commencement to receive a degree. Their self-esteem, confidence, and optimism were greatly enhanced as they embarked on their next step in life.

These students achieved success by riding the challenging waves and coming out of the educational process as mature adults. They enabled themselves to remain on the stage of life and perform as equals and do their part to influence public perception about people and their disabilities. All of us human beings are given free will to overcome adversity and challenges because of an internal drive that defines who we are.

It was August of 1963 when Martin Luther King made his "I have a dream" speech. As millions of people witnessed his statements and prayers, the world on that day changed forever. People became more aware of and focused on civil rights for people of color. I too have a dream that one day people with disabilities will be able to live quality lives where misconceptions and biases fall away, and society accepts who we are and recognizes our gifts and talents.

Chapter 18

Coming Full Circle

To close the life journey described in this book, I'd like to comment on just a couple more things related to the prism of disability.

In social situations or family gatherings, especially when it is my turn to share something about what I'm doing—maybe to describe a project I've taken on, or an enjoyable outing at a restaurant, or a travel adventure I've just returned from—a common response I hear is, "You are amazing." I acknowledge the compliment, and usually nothing more is said about me being amazing. But I often ask myself what in the other person's eyes made me amazing. Compliments are wonderful and they enhance the ego of the recipient. However, I believe that more often than not, this compliment comes from a mindset where my visual disability is a factor. I have accomplished many things in my life, and in many circumstances being visually impaired has either hindered or helped me. But would I have been called "amazing" if I had done the same things or lived the same life without this disability?

Throughout my career as a counselor, I always tried to look at the entire person as I developed a course of study or rehabilitation plan for a disabled student. The word "amazing" didn't enter my mind. If clients succeeded at their goals, I thought about their excellent skills and behaviors rather than how amazing they were. But the word "amazing" is used loosely and easily by those who rarely interact with people with disabilities, and who marvel at their unexpected accomplishments. Having said this, I need to add that my buddy Jay often tells me how amazed he is at what I can do. I always thank him for saying that, but I don't think I'm amazing. I take his and other people's comments in stride, but I tell myself that I did what I had to do for my own well-being and the expectations I had set for myself.

Another question I receive is "Would you have lived your life differently if you had not been born with a visual disability?" Granted, this question is usually asked by someone trying to learn more about disability issues.

I cannot offer a yes or no answer. Surely my life would have been very different in that I would drive a car and might have chosen a different career. I am sure my outlook on life would have been different in that my personal attributes alone (without a disability) would have affected how I came across to others. But these factors are not worth speculating about. The person I have become in seventy-six years has evolved in part from having a visual disability and from what I have been able to do with my life—bad or good—by not allowing my disability to define me or take full control of my life. The hardships I experienced and the ways I dealt with adversity have empowered me. Those of us with a disabling condition must take on its challenges and learn and grow from the inconvenience. Everyone faces adversity. As someone surely has said, "Blindness is not so bad; it all depends on how you look at it."

My disability did not stop me from getting married and having a family. It does not prevent me from attending baseball games, movies, and concerts. My friendships were not based on the severity of my disability, but rather on the person I became and what I offer in my interactions with others. When I visit my immediate family, my disability is not the center of discussion; it is buried somewhere in the subconscious of our souls. This is why we should always put the person first and the disability second when we describe someone who is marginalized by a physical or mental impairment. As I see it, how we address our adversity is how we mature and become better human beings—disabled or not.

I do not think it's insensitive of people to ask the above question. It offers an opportunity for the person with the disability to talk about their lifestyle and situation with the person asking the question. The discussion that follows can enlighten both parties.

Another question I often hear, and one I have given considerable thought to, is, "In your view, are people with disabilities any better off now than they were seventy-five years ago?"

The short answer must be yes, given the Americans with Disabilities Act, along with advancements in technology and medical research. People get around in automated wheelchairs, drive cars with adaptable hand controls, and take advantage of diverse public transportation resources. Telephone relay systems and real-time captions on TV and in theaters have greatly enhanced communication for the hearing impaired. Great efforts are being made to address the social and educational issues of people with autism and learning disabilities. The Special Olympics makes it possible for those with developmental disabilities to showcase their physical prowess. Even more encouraging is that a U.S. census report states that as late as 2017, there were 438,000 students with disabilities enrolled in undergraduate programs across the country. Education is power, and it is essential for the disabled to obtain a certificate or college degree if they are to experience the American dream of living a quality life and feeling satisfied that their efforts will enhance the social good. It is not always the disability that impedes our success, but how we decide to confront our problems and use our talents to assert our place in life.

A recent incident while I was working as a line manager at a Giants game in San Francisco illustrates this necessity. Customers were walking up to the Marina gate to show their tickets and enter the stadium. As is always the case, a couple approached me to ask how they could get to the will-call window to pick up tickets that were on hold. As I began to offer directions, my boss walked over and interrupted me and began helping the customer by giving them the same information I had been providing. I walked away feeling angry and upset. My first thought was, "Why do they need me out here to assist people, if the supervisor is going to handle these matters? Should I confront my boss, or am I overreacting?" A feeling of inadequacy crept into my mind. "It's my disability that's causing my boss to act that way," I thought. "What can I do to handle this situation and feel good about it?"

As I was contemplating my options, my boss walked over to me and apologized. He was gracious and sincere and regretted his actions. The point here is this: If we are to overcome people's misconceptions and biases, we owe it to ourselves to remain objective about our experiences, step back, and evaluate the bigger picture before passing judgment on ourselves or the individuals causing the problem. My boss's actions, good or bad, had little if anything to do with my disability. He forgot his manners and projected himself into the situation as a supervisor, without looking at the whole picture. I reacted before I had time to think through all the dynamics. If we as disabled folks want to sustain our equality in society, we must strive to retain our objectivity in challenging moments. Then we will become more assertive and intelligent about how we respond to people. Strength comes from adversity, and this incident reminded me that we must roll with the punches. We are people first, just like our neighbors and coworkers, all of whom are just as vulnerable as we are.

Finally, I believe this small incident adds fuel to my argument that people living with a disability are better off today because, believe it or not, the average citizen has moments where they look at us not from a standpoint of pity or inequality but rather as individuals who can act for ourselves in spite of our marginal status. All of us who are disabled must in our own way strive to send the message that we claim our place in society not because of our disabilities but because of our diversity and God-given talents.

My aim in this book has been to bring you the reader to a closer understanding of life as seen through the prism of disability. As Winston Churchill said, "Success is not final. Failure is not fatal. It is the courage to continue that counts." Churchill also reminds us, "If you are going through hell, keep going." So long as we are alive, we must filter out the challenging moments, learn from the adversity, and move forward with optimism to resolve circumstances that cause us dismay.

I believe my life story has meaning not just because of what I have been able to achieve, but also because I have been fortunate to encounter many wonderful people in my life. I have been nurtured by these interactions. As I recall sitting on the laps of family members as a child; sharing good times with my wife, children, and grandchildren; hashing over the highs and lows of the San Francisco Giants with coworkers at Oracle Park; and many other experiences, I cannot describe the feelings of contentment and happiness these moments have brought me. I have been made whole by listening to and learning from the people who have come in and out of my life.

One thing is certain: Whatever direction life takes me, the experience will be accompanied by the wisdom I have gained. As David Brooks, the writer and PBS news analyst eloquently states, "Wisdom isn't a body of information. It's the moral quality of knowing what you don't know and figuring out a way to handle your ignorance, uncertainty, and limitation."

I vividly recall sitting one afternoon with my son Michael in the forest near the Oregon Coast. It was a beautiful sunny day, I could hear the birds singing, and there was a stillness that always puts me in a reflective mood. In that natural setting, Michael shared his vision of life. "Dad, I love being here in Oregon working on this small farm. I see myself as a person who tries to improve the environment for all of us. It gives me great satisfaction to use what nature has given us to grow fruits and vegetables and terrace the land in a natural way where erosion is not caused by man's mistakes." My son at age twenty-six, in his love for his job, was teaching me wisdom in areas I'd never considered, like ecology and ways of farming that respect the earth.

So, here I am, attempting to pass along to you my life story full of adventures and perspectives that might elicit a bit of wisdom on your part to approach things differently and constructively. We are continually adapting in life, seeking those special moments free of adversity, that allow us to spread our metaphorical wings to where life is good and the world is at our feet. We experience this euphoria at numerous times in our lives, whether it's when we propose and get a yes from our spouse-to-be, or when our first child is born, or we achieve a goal, or just sit at home and cuddle with our children and grandchildren. In these special moments, the world is full of the good things that make life precious and wonderful. To quote Henry David Thoreau, "Heaven is under our feet as well as over our heads."

I never imagined in all my life that I would attempt to write a book about my life. There is no doubt that those of you who know me as an acquaintance, friend, or relative have influenced me in such a way that all of us together have made something special happen here. At the Chase Center where I work, team spirit is the theme and everyone, from top management to part-time workers, is made to feel part of the company mission. By reading this book, you automatically become part of my team. So, my enthusiasm for living a quality life is at a high level, as I add another story to the billions of stories that have ever been written. A Dutch proverb says that "He who is outside his door already has the hardest part of his journey behind him." Writing this narrative has brought me closer to opening that door. May God bless all of you for spending your time reading these pages.

I leave you with a wonderful quotation from Michelle Obama in her book *Belonging:* "I grew up with a disabled dad in a too-small house with not much money in a starting-to-fail neighborhood, and I also grew up surrounded by love and music in a diverse city in a country where an education can take you far. I had nothing or I had everything. It depends on which way you want to tell it."

Many of her words in *Belonging* reflect thoughts I shared in this narrative but are framed in ways that expand the meaning of diversity, showing time and time again how enriched are lives can become if we continue to strive toward excellence.

Appendix: Agency Resources

The California Department of Rehabilitation supported me through my college years by paying for part of my tuition, books and supplies, and reader support. There are countless other social services programs and specialized agencies available if we make the contacts that will open doors for us. It starts with special education programs in public schools and later community college and university support services that offer special accommodations to make college degrees accessible and viable. People not inclined or able to attend college might opt for trade and vocational schools. Monetary assistance could come from Social Security programs or state employment development departments offering financial options to accomplish training objectives.

Listed below are a few agencies and programs that serve people with disabilities locally and at the national level. Check them out to see what support is available.

American Action Fund for Blind Children and Adults
https://actionfund.org/

American Foundation for the Blind https://www.afb.org/

American Mental Health Counselors Association
https://www.amhca.org/home

American Printing House for the Blind https://www.aph.org/

California Committee on Employment of People with Disabilities (CCEPD) https://www.dor.ca.gov/Home/Ccepd

California Department of Developmental Services (DDS)
https://www.dds.ca.gov/

California Department of Rehabilitation (DOR)
https://www.dor.ca.gov/

California Employment Development Department LEAP Program for qualified disabled applicants seeking state employment
https://edd.ca.gov/en/about_edd/leap_program/

California State Chancellor's Office; community college system, State of California https://www.cccco.edu/

Center for Independent Living (Berkeley, California)
https://www.centerforindependentliving.org

Disability Rights Education and Defense Fund
https://dredf.org/

LightHouse for the Blind and Visually Impaired
(San Francisco, California) https://lighthouse-sf.org/

People First, a national organization for people with learning difficulties https://peoplefirstltd.com/

Vista Center for the Blind and Visually Impaired
https://vistacenter.org/

National laws pertaining to the rights of persons with disabilities (title and full disclosure):

Americans with Disabilities Act of 1990
https://www.eeoc.gov/americans-disabilities-act-1990-original-text

Individuals with Disabilities Education Act, which afforded all school age children with disabilities access to the nation's public-school system https://sites.ed.gov/idea/

Rehabilitation Act of 1972
https://openlibrary.org/books/OL5391745M/Rehabilitation_act_of_1972

Acknowledgments

When my granddaughter Annabella was five years old, she often said to me: "Grandpa, we are friends forever, even when you pass into the next world." In that spirit, I want to acknowledge many people who I will appreciate forever for the ways in which they have enriched my life with their presence, goodwill, and love, whether we met in school, college, on the job, or elsewhere.

Teachers from grade and junior high school: Dr. Buell, Mrs. Nunes, Mrs. Wright-Groelle (school librarian and now a friend), Mr. English, and Mr. Salzberry. Oakland Tech teachers: Mr. Cuttitta, Mrs. Stokes, Mr. Grimes, Mr. McKay, and Mr. Rosen. Robert Campbell, administrator of the reader support program at the School for the Blind.

Also at Oakland Tech: Fellow students Sharon Welch, a close friend; Rich Carle, Cheryl Chung, Anita Donchi, Bob Drago, and many others; and Claire Johnston, one of my readers who took me under her wing.

At the College of San Mateo: Dr. Charles Height, my Western Civilization instructor; Mr. Richmond, my academic counselor.

At Santa Clara University: History professors Timothy O'Keefe and George Giacomoni. Rev. Father Tennant Wright, for his supreme kindness and for looking upon his neighbors with grace and goodwill, and for the special mass he said for my wife and me before the birth of our first child. Reverend Father John Hynes, Dean of Liberal Studies. Dianne, who always had a kind word for me. Cathleen, from Deerfield Illinois. Bob Spence, on the SCU baseball team. Ron

Brutico, who got me backstage to meet Ray Charles. Chuck Conway, a fellow graduate, and his oldest son, Cloyce, my godson. Ron Sutter and Bruce Graham, my roommates. Cathleen Erickson, reader.

Mr. Wally Stewart, teacher at Marina Junior High School. Betty Ross, social worker, fellow graduate student, and reader who helped me study for (and pass, I'm sure) exams for my Master's degree, and now my friend as well as godmother to my daughter Monica. Ernest White, program administrator of the Marin County Office of Education.

At the Department of Rehabilitation in San Jose, California: Special praise for my coworkers Nell Jenkins, John Crane, Phil Su, and my supervisor Jack Brazil, who always took time to listen to my concerns and suggest resources for my clients. The secretarial support from wonderful ladies including Barbara, Ellen, Jerri, and Hazel. John Crane, who inspired me with his ability to recover from serious injury and comforted me when I faced severe adversity. My friend Rick from the DMV, who ran 5 and 10K races with me. I am also grateful for the enduring friendship of coworker Bonnie Evans and her late husband Mike.

People who supported me through some career adversity, including Father Martin Maroney as well as Gina, Bill, Connie, and others whose names I don't remember.

At Victor Valley College: Shirley and Chuck Peterson, who consistently took me under their wing. Layne Marshall, Dean of Student Services and of special support to me, and his wife Paulette.

In Monterey: Anna Foglia, Cathalene Nolan, who began a conversation with me during a time of flooded streets in Monterey that led to a twenty-year friendship. Greg Bearsdley, who offered support when I needed it most. Job coach Neila.

At Evergreen College in San Jose: Harvey Gipson, who drove twenty minutes out of his way to give me a ride to our work in San

Jose and helped me complete repetitious employment applications. Myron Washington, who made sure I reached the commuter train on time and helped me with adaptive technology. Marianne, speech pathologist, who taught me what a program coordinator must do to be an effective leader. Liz, program secretary, who went out of her way to assist me with job priorities. Catherine Canpisi, Director of the Department of Rehabilitation, with whom I cohosted a day of training activities. The business program dean and the wonderful VP of student services offered consultation and encouragement that propelled me to keep moving forward. Phil Frey, fellow shuttle bus passenger who invited me into his life and made me feel like a member of his family. A beacon of light in my life, Phil passed on unexpectedly in 2016. I cherish his friendship and the good times with him and his family.

At Napa Valley College: My predecessor, Catherine Brown, who had done a great job as the Workability III program administrator. Malia, program secretary, and Linda, program tutor/basic skills instructor. Betty, Margo, Gwen, Laura Lynn, Rebecca, Marcy, Jerry, Bill, Mark, Ron, and countless others whose names I don't recall supported me in ways that added to what I could implement for my students. Stephanie Burns, Biology instructor. John Adams, DOR counselor. Dean Ehlen, Machine Shop instructor. Rebecca Scott, college librarian, Gwen Kell, counselor, and Mark Martin. Oscar DeHaro, Vice President of Student Services. Chris McCarthy, President/Superintendent of NVC who always made time in his busy schedule to attend my meetings.

At Guest Services for the San Francisco Giants: Alexis Lustbader, who initially interviewed me for a job; Jeff Kuiper; Bill, Marilyn, and Don, who've become my friends on the job.

Pat Pepper, recruiter of volunteers at the Upper Peninsula Symphony League, Vonya Morris who often provides a ride to meetings.

Other special people: Tony Fletcher, director of Enchanted Hills Camp (owned by LightHouse for the Blind and Visually Impaired) in Napa, California, for his enthusiasm, kindness, and friendship, and for the community advocacy, awareness, and success he brings to this unique camping experience. Liz Wright-Groelle, my longtime friend from School for the Blind, who often invites me to the symphony. Breann, a worker at the local Trader Joe's, whose helpful service when I asked for help finding food items has led to friendship. My friends Lucy and Rick, who I traveled with on my first cruise to Alaska. Cookie and Dennis Murphy, who I met while working at Blind Services in Nevada, where Dennis served me well as a carpool connection and catalyst to enhance my social calendar; we remain friends today. I also love their daughters, Keli and Keri.

My special friends: Jay Henderick and Larry Holsen; the three of us form a brotherhood I am blessed to be part of. Also Jay's partner Karen and Larry's partner Joann, both of whom have become dear friends; Joann's daughter, Sandy, and her husband Elliott Levin, a special friend whose medical knowledge as a former respiratory therapist helped me at a critical time. Jack and Hannelore Banks, neighbors who have been a tremendous help to my mother and me for many years. Charlanne Wheaton and her mother, Katherine Myrovich, who introduced me to my future wife.

For assistance in creating this book: Words cannot explain the appreciation and respect I have for Darlene Frank as editor of my manuscript. Her expertise and open-minded approach led to a narrative that captures the essence of my life's journey. She has been an integral part of the team throughout the book production process. Special credit to Cynthia Clifford for proofreading and for offering her perspective on disability issues and language. Her input enhanced my thoughts and words. My appreciation for Deanna Washington, book designer and artist, for her excellent work in creating a printed book that offers sighted readers an enjoyable and easy-to-access reading experience.

Finally, I want to acknowledge and give thanks for key people who have put up with me through the years and in their own way propelled me through the process of bringing this narrative to life: My grandmother Mary, my mother, my wife Eileen, all my children and grandchildren, my sister Marianne, my cousin Sylvia Vaiana, my good friends Bonnie Evans, Anna Foglia, Rebecca Scott, Lucy Reyes, Margaret Eastham, Liz Groelle, Jay Henderick, Larry Holsen, Rick Reyes, Steve Hom, John Crane, Chuck Conway, Phil Frey, and so many others who I by no means intend to neglect. I thank my lucky stars for the life paths that led me to all of you and how you have enriched my life on so many levels.

About the Author

THOMAS DANA has lived an extraordinary life despite being blind as a result of a medical treatment administered to approximately ten thousand babies born prematurely between the early 1940s and mid-1950s. He graduated from Oakland Tech high school in 1964, earned a BA in history from the University of Santa Clara, a secondary teaching credential from the University of San Francisco, and a Master's degree in counseling psychology. He became a vocational rehabilitation counselor and spent many years as a community college coordinator of disabled student services programs. His memoir, *Looking Through the Prism: Navigating Life with a Visual Disability*, challenges the reader (disabled or not) to take responsibility for accepting and understanding the plight of the marginalized in a way that will help bridge the social gap between the disabled and the general public. Tom is a husband, father of five and grandfather of six, and has been a devoted marathon runner for many years. He lives in San Mateo, California.

Made in the USA
Monee, IL
10 January 2023

21609346R00111